May God ... in your divine ministry.

The Power Vested in Us
Discover How Much God Has Invested in You

JASON M. SILVER

DEDICATION

I would like to dedicate this book to all the men and women who throughout history have stepped out into a life of faith and obedience to God, and saw the impossible made possible through Him!

CONTENTS

ACKNOWLEDGMENTS

I would like to thank my all-loving and kind Heavenly Father, and His son Jesus Christ for choosing to bear the Cross in my place. Without Him I would not have breath to breathe and hands to write.

I would also like to thank my ever-loving and supportive wife Patricia and my three children, Judah, Rebecca and Cherith. You all are an obvious blessing from God. And last but not least my present Church family, Kimberley Foursquare Fellowship, thank you for loving and supporting us throughout these years.

PREFACE

Even before Adam ever became the apple of His Daddy's eye, or a thought in His infinite mind, the Father's desire was to be bound to His creation in intimate relationship. That is for Him to be in us, and us in Him. Jesus exemplified this while on earth. We see this when we hear Him say these words, **"I and the Father are one..." (John 10:30)** This intimacy being like that in a marriage, where, **"...the two shall become one flesh." (Ephesians 5:31)** Although with God, Who is spirit, we become one in and by the Spirit.

Adam had this type of intimacy with God in the Garden, but ate from the forbidden tree, and His spiritual union and fellowship with God, were broken. And because anyone of us would have done the same thing, we too are born into this fallen world in a fallen state. Yes, Romans 5:19 says that, **"...through the disobedience of the one man the many were made sinners..."** Due to the fact that God cannot dwell in the presence of sin, He could no longer dwell within us, but only among us. However this was not God's best, He wanted back that intimacy with His Creation.

So in His wisdom, He made a way through the sacrifice of His only Son. A way that would bridge the separation between us and restore divine intimacy once again. **"Yet to all who received him, to those who believed in his name, he gave the right to become children of God, children born not of natural descent, nor of human decision or a husband's will, but born of God." (John 1:12-13)**

And, **"Do you not know that your body is a temple of the Holy Spirit, who is in you, whom you have received from God? You are not your own; you were bought at a price. Therefore honor God with your body." (1 Corinthians 6:19-20)**

In His immeasurable and often misunderstood wisdom, the Lord had a plan. A plan, that to the world; would seem foolish. **"For the message of the cross is foolishness to those who are perishing, but to us who are being saved it is the power of God. (1 Corinthians 1:18)** He has chosen us less than perfect vessels by His Son and through His Spirit, to present the power of His Presence to a lost and dying world that so desperately needs Him.

My prayer is that as you read this book, God by His Spirit, will reveal to you the power of the treasure He has deposited on the inside of all who have received Christ by His Spirit. **"For you have an anointing from the Holy One..." (1 John 2:20) and "You are a temple of the Holy Spirit..." (1 Corinthians 6:19)**

To be a temple of the Living God is no light responsibility, but along with other things, demands us as the carrying vessels to be broken. Yes, broken of our own will and desires, to follow His, and His alone. I believe that if the Christian life seems boring to you right now, you are probably not broken. For to be broken is exciting, and powerful!! Brokenness appears weak, however; it is the things that appear weak that will confound the wise! May God Bless you as you journey with me into The Power Vested in Us.

CHAPTER ONE
The Old Vessel

**And let them construct a sanctuary for Me, that I may
dwell among them.**
Exodus 25:8

I don't know if God could make it clearer than this. He
wanted to be with His creation in such a way that even
though we were now fallen short of His glory, He still made
a way for Him to be among us. We see in Exodus 25:8-22
God commanding the Israelites to construct an ark in which
God Himself could dwell. The Lord had them fashion it with
beautiful materials according to His strict specifications. It
was then later on to be assembled by Bezalel, the son of Uri
and others the Lord put with Him. (Exodus 31:1-7)

In Exodus 25:8-22, God mentions more than once, **"...in
the ark you shall put the <u>testimony</u> which I shall give
you."** You will see why later on. Now, you'll need to bear
with me for the first few chapters, as I will be using a lot of
passages to lay out a scriptural basis for this book.

THE CONTENTS OF THE OLD VESSEL

We are told in Hebrews 9:4 just what items were in the
Ark of the Covenant. They were, **"A golden jar holding the
manna, and Aaron's rod which budded, and the stone
tablets of the covenant."**

THE MANNA

"Moses said, "This is what the LORD has commanded: 'Take an omer of manna and keep it for the generations to come, so they can see the bread I gave you to eat in the desert when I brought you out of Egypt.'"

So Moses said to Aaron, "Take a jar and put an omer of manna in it. Then place it before the Lord to be kept for the generations to come." As the Lord commanded Moses, Aaron   put the manna in front of the Testimony, so that it might be kept. (Exodus 16:32-35)

AARON'S ROD THAT BUDDED

This was to prove to those in the rebellion against Moses' and Aaron's leadership, led by Korah, that God had truly chosen Aaron to represent and lead the Levites as His chosen priesthood. (Numbers 16:3) **"Now it came about on the next day that Moses went into the tent of the testimony; and behold, the rod of Aaron for the house of Levi had sprouted and put forth buds and produced blossoms, and it bore ripe almonds. Moses then brought out all the rods from the presence of the Lord to all the sons of Israel; and they looked, and each man took his rod. But the Lord said to Moses, "Put back the rod of Aaron before the testimony to be kept as a sign against the rebels, that you may put an end to their grumbling against Me, so that they should not die." Thus Moses did; just as the Lord had commanded him, so he did."** (Numbers 17:8-11)

THE STONE TABLETS

"Moses took the Testimony and placed it in the ark..." (Exodus 40:20) As I referred to before this was the first thing God commanded to be placed in the Ark.

According to procedure for covenants in those days, the terms of the covenant were to be recorded in writing, and stored safely. This interestingly enough, is still how we do it today. I am reminded of the awesomeness of God's word, when I see the importance He stressed on having it be the first item put in the ark. The scripture that comes to my mind is Isaiah 40:8. It says, **"The grass of the field withers, and the flower fades, but the Word of our God stands forever."**

Later on we will look at how each one of the items placed in the ark back then, relates to the Church today. I think you will be quite amazed!

HIS PRESENCE AMONG THE PEOPLE

"And Joshua said, "By this you shall know that the living God is <u>among</u> you, and that He will assuredly dispossess from before you the Canaanite, the Hittite, the Hivite, the Perizzite, the Girgashite, the Amorite, and the Jebusite. Behold, the ark of the covenant of the Lord of all the earth is crossing over ahead of you into the Jordan. Now then, take for yourselves twelve men from the tribes of Israel, one man for each tribe. And it shall come about when the soles of the feet of the priests who carry the ark of the Lord, the Lord of all the earth, shall rest in the waters of the Jordan, the waters of the Jordan shall be cut off, and the waters which are flowing down from above shall stand in one heap.

" So it came about when the people set out from their tents to cross the Jordan with the priests carrying the ark of the covenant before the people, and when those who carried the ark came into the Jordan, and the feet of the priests carrying the ark were dipped in the edge of the water (for the Jordan overflows all its banks all the days of

harvest), that the waters which were flowing down from above stood and rose up in one heap, a great distance away at Adam, the city that is beside Zarethan; and those which were flowing down toward the sea of the Arabah, the Salt Sea, were completely cut off.

So the people crossed opposite Jericho. And the priests who carried the ark of the covenant of the Lord stood firm on dry ground in the middle of the Jordan while all Israel crossed on dry ground, until the entire nation had finished crossing the Jordan." (Joshua 3:7-17)

Then we see Israel come to the great walled city of Jericho. And an angel of the Lord tells Joshua, "See, I have delivered Jericho into your hands, along with its king and its fighting men. March around the city once, with all the armed men. Do this for six days. Have seven priests carry trumpets of rams' horns in front of the ark. On the seventh day, march around the city seven times, with the priests blowing the trumpets. When you hear them sound a long blast on the trumpets, have all the people give a loud shout; then the wall of the city will collapse and the people will go up, every man straight in." (Joshua 6:2-5)

These were very powerful things that God's presence in the ark was allowing the Israelites to do! However, the problem is, that they began to look to these miraculous provisions, rather than to the Provider of them. Yes, the very thing the first generation ended in, did this next generation begin. The Lord wanted the affections of his people, as any good Father would desire from a child. But they continually took for granted His provision, all the while ignoring His presence.

In 1 Samuel 4 we begin to see the consequence of presuming God's provision, without a pursuit of His presence. **"Now the Israelites went out to fight against the**

Philistines. The Israelites camped at Ebenezer, and the Philistines at Aphek. The Philistines deployed their forces to meet Israel, and as the battle spread, Israel was defeated by the Philistines, who killed about four thousand of them on the battlefield. When the soldiers returned to camp, the elders of Israel asked, "Why did the Lord bring defeat upon us today before the Philistines? Let us bring the ark of the Lord's covenant from Shiloh, so that <u>it may go with us and save us</u> from the hand of our enemies." (1 Samuel 4:1-3) Now I want to look at the last part of that passage.

What was their response to the loss of the battle to the Philistines? This is what they said. **"Why did the Lord bring defeat upon us today before the Philistines?"** Now watch this... **"Let us bring the ark of the Lord's covenant from Shiloh, so that it may go with us and save us from the hand of our enemies."**

The most important and vital thing about the ark; was that God's presence was in it. Yet Israel began to look to a wooden box for its help rather than to God. What they had forgotten was that the ark was made for God, not the other way around. I wonder how many times in our lives do we see God only in His provisions for us.

If the only time you think of God, and seek His face, is when you need His provision; you might want to repent, and reevaluate your relationship with Him. I know, I've had to do this many times in my walk with God. You're probably thinking, "Why such a strong word as repent?"Because God commanded us to love and worship Him with all our hearts, not the things He does for us, or gives us. In fact whatever would rob our complete affections away from God would be an idol.

I believe this is why we are unable to be find the ark to this day. It would become to those possessing it, an idol. Israel's affections, witnessed by their own words, began to lean towards the ark, rather than to the One for which it was created, for their provision of victory in battle.

God saw this and He could not allow them to look to the vessel, but only to Him. So here's what happened. **"So the Philistines fought, and the Israelites were defeated and every man fled to his tent. The slaughter was very great; Israel lost thirty thousand foot soldiers. The ark of God was captured, and Eli's two sons, Hophni and Phinehas, died." (1 Samuel 4:10-11)**

I think of those who pursue entering into full time ministry. And I've even heard some say, "This is my gifting, I can do it. I can see myself using my gifting to do it." Yes, I too believe that, "A man's gift makes room for him, and brings him before great men. (Proverbs 18:16) But we must not trust the gift over the Giver. Every time we do this, it will spell trouble.

Now, let's look at some further scripture showing the power of His presence in the Ark. **"After the Philistines had captured the ark of God, they took it from Ebenezer to Ashdod. Then they carried the ark into Dagon's temple and set it beside Dagon. When the people of Ashdod rose early the next day, there was Dagon, fallen on his face on the ground before the ark of the Lord!**

So they took Dagon and put him back in his place. But the following morning when they rose, there was Dagon, fallen on his face on the ground before the ark of the Lord! His head and hands had been broken off and were lying on the threshold; only his body remained. That is why to this day neither the priests of Dagon nor any others who enter Dagon's temple at Ashdod step on the threshold." (1 Samuel 5:1-5)

This event has always left me in amazement. I mean, how could the Philistines witness this awesome power of the True Living God, yet still not turn to Him? Even their false god made of stone fell prostrate in worship before the Ark twice, and was broken. Yet the Philistines still claimed Dagon to be their god. And then we read on further in 1 Samuel, and we find Israel again in such a short time, giving themselves over to false idols. And how much more of God's power had they experienced personally, and not just heard about?

"They called their priest's and diviner's and they said, "Why do you harden your hearts as the Egyptians and Pharaoh did? When he treated them harshly, did they not send the Israelites out so they could go on their way?"(1 Samuel 6:6)

Even these uncircumcised priests heard of the God of Israel's power, yet did not submit to it. Wow, this baffles me!! This scripture comes to mind, **"For they exchanged the truth of God for a lie, and worshiped and served the created rather than the Creator, who is blessed forever. Amen. (Romans 1:25)**

We can see the Ark had many great exploits surrounding it, from God's people gaining victory in battle, to ungodly people feeling the weight and curse of having it in possession, and godly households being blessed in storing it, such as Obed-edom. (1Chronicles 13:14) All these felt and experienced the power of His presence among them.

It truly is amazing what God did among His people, and ever since my Sunday school days, I love to hear the accounts. But this wasn't all that the Lord had for us. It wasn't His best. To be among His people was more of an acquainted relationship, not one of intimacy. However, He would now make a way where there seemed to be no way.

He would do the very thing that for men, was impossible, but with Him was absolutely possible.

He would make a way to live within His people, and restore divine intimacy. He would literally invest Himself in us.

The old way wasn't working. **"Therefore the former regulation was set aside because it was weak and useless (for the law made nothing perfect), and a better hope is introduced, by which we <u>draw near</u> to God. (Hebrews 7:18-19)**

"By calling this covenant "new," he has made the first one obsolete; and what is obsolete and aging will soon disappear. (Hebrews 8:13)

As a matter of fact, the Law came to show us that we couldn't do it, but only God could. Any other way without Him, simply would not work. So God made a promise to His people, that he would make a new and better way. A way unlike the Law, but that would come through the Law. Concerning this, Paul the Apostle said, **"For through the Law I died to the Law, that I might live to God. (Galatians 2:19)** The law killed him, rather his old way of living. That is, his own ability to fulfill the law. So that once dead to his own ability to fulfill the Law, he could now depend on Christ who Himself fulfilled the whole law with love.

But hold on now I'm getting ahead of myself. In the next chapter we will look at God's promise to His people, to send the Messiah. And how many looked *forward* to His coming, to restore the hearts of the children to the Father. Just as we now look *back* to His coming, and the finished work of the cross.

THE PROMISE OF SOMETHING NEW

"The time is coming," declares the LORD, "when I will make a new covenant with the house of Israel and with the house of Judah." (Jeremiah 31:31)

From what we just discussed, we see that there had to come something or someone else. One who was different from us less than perfect vessels, and from God who is perfect; sharing in the flesh, but without the sinful reproductive seed of Adam. **"Since the children have flesh and blood, he too shared in their humanity so that by his death he might destroy him who holds the power of death-that is, the devil and free those who all their lives were held in slavery by their fear of death." (Hebrews 2:14-15)**

This is why the doctrine of the Immaculate Conception is so vital to uphold. Mary did not lie with a man descended from sinful Adam. No, she was overshadowed by the Holy Spirit. **"The angel answered, 'The Holy Spirit will come upon you, and the power of the Most High will <u>overshadow</u> you. So the holy One to be born will be called the Son of God.'" (Luke 1:35-36)**

There had to come to us, one who could bridge the gap, and restore the intimacy to the Creator and His creation. The only One who could destroy, in the flesh, that which caused this broken relationship, sin. He came in flesh to destroy sin in the flesh. Jesus fulfilled the Law and all the commandments in one act of selfless obedience. Thus He fulfilled the greatest commandment; being love.

God once again came among us, in and through His Son Jesus.

Emmanuel, God is with us. He came to show us that the Way to restored relationship with God, was and is still only through Him.

"Greater love has no one than this that one lay down his life for his friends. (John 15:13-14) "…Love therefore is the fulfillment of the law." (Romans 13:10)

THE PROPHETIC PROMISE

All throughout scripture, to those who were prophets, kings, and those who feared the Lord, He spoke of the coming Messiah. Yes the One, the Anointed One that is Jesus Christ to be exact. His purpose on earth would be to destroy the works of the devil allowed in through Adam, and restore God's dream of Eden. "The Son of God appeared for this purpose, that He might destroy the works of the devil." (1 John 3:8)

You see one of the first works of the devil was in the Garden. He worked quite hard to convince Eve that if she ate from the tree she would "…surely not die." (Genesis 3:4) Adam and Eve were the first of Satan's killings, for they died spiritually. For the Devil comes to steal, kill, and destroy.

But Jesus was promised to come and bring life where death had come in. "The devil comes only to steal and kill and destroy; I have come that they may have life, and have it to the full." (John 10:10)

A FEW OF MANY

I've chosen three prophecies in no particular order, out of the 1093 prophetic utterances of the promise of the New Way. Each one has the New Testament fulfillment to the Old Testament promise.

Born of A Virgin

"Therefore the Lord himself will give you a sign: The virgin will be with child and will give birth to a son and will call Him Emmanuel." (Isaiah7: 14)

"This is how the birth of Jesus Christ came about: his mother Mary was pledged to be married to Joseph, but before they came together, she was found to be with child through the Holy Spirit." (Matthew 1:18)

He Shall be Called a Nazarene

"...for the child shall be a Nazarite unto God." (Judges 13:5)

"And he came and dwelt in a city called Nazareth: that it might be fulfilled which was spoken by the prophets, He shall be called a Nazarene." (Matthew 2:23)

He Was Hated Without Reason

"Those who hate me without reason outnumber the hairs of my head; many are my enemies without cause, those who seek to destroy me. I am forced to restore what I did not steal." (Psalm 69:4)

"He who hates me hates my Father as well. If I had not done among them what no one else did, they would not be guilty of sin. But now they have seen these miracles, and yet they have hated both My Father and me. But this is to fulfill what is written in their Law: 'They hated me without reason.'" (John 15:23-2)

Now there are still 1090 prophecies left, but for the sake of time, and space in this book, we will rely on these scriptures as validity to Christ being prophesied about in the Old Testament. You see the only thing that separated us from God, was sin. It had to be removed for us to move ahead in relationship with Him. However, there is no removal of sins, without the shedding of blood.

"In fact we can say that under the old agreement almost everything was cleansed by sprinkling it with blood, and without the shedding of blood there is no forgiveness of sins." (Hebrews 9:22)

In order for the old law to be fulfilled, this had to be part of the promise. We could only have restored intimacy made available once again through blood sacrifice. **"But now in Christ Jesus you who once were far away have been <u>brought near</u> through the blood of Christ."(Ephesians 2:13)**

A BETTER COVENANT HOLDS BETTER PROMISE

"That is why Christ said as he came into the world, "O God, the blood of bulls and goats cannot satisfy you, so you have made ready this body of mine for me to lay as a sacrifice upon your altar. You were not satisfied with the animal sacrifices, slain and burnt before you as offerings for sin. Then I said, 'See, I have come to do your will, to lay down my life, just as the Scriptures said that I would.'"

After Christ said this about not being satisfied with the various sacrifices and offerings required under the old system, he then added, "Here I am. I have come to give my life."He cancels the first system in favor of a far better one. Under this new plan we have been forgiven and made clean by Christ's dying for us once and for all. Under the

old agreement the priests stood before the altar day after day offering sacrifices that could never take away our sins.

But Christ gave himself to God for our sins as one sacrifice for all time and then sat down in the place of highest honor at God's right hand, waiting for his enemies to be laid under his feet. For by that one offering he made forever perfect in the sight of God all those whom he is making holy." (Hebrews 10:5-14)

Oh what a promise fulfilled in Christ Jesus!! What a powerful atonement! What a glorious freedom bought by the blood of the Son of the Living God!!

You know as I read the scripture above, I'm reminded of another scripture. One that at first glance appears that God may be contradicting Himself. It has also perhaps left many with a works based mentality, feeling helpless in the ability to fulfill it. And that scripture is Matthew 5:48, it says, **"Be perfect, therefore, as your heavenly Father is perfect."** I've asked God myself many times, "Father I can't seem to do it..." And now I find the Lord saying, "Son, you're right!!" "You can't do it..." "...because Jesus already did!!"

Look at the last part in the above passage of Hebrews. "**For by that one offering He made forever perfect in the sight of God all those whom he is making holy.**"

2 Corinthians 5:21 says, **"He made Him who knew no sin (Jesus) to be sin on our behalf, that we might become the righteousness of God in Christ."** So therefore, **"...if anyone is in Christ, he is a new creation; the old has gone, the new has come! (2 Corinthians 5:17)** Hallelujah, we are now perfect as the Father is perfect. That is, in our new man, the new creation!! And that is if we are in Christ, by receiving Him into us. Jesus has therefore qualified us to be perfect

vessels to carry the Presence of God, for God is Holy and cannot dwell in imperfection (sin). But Jesus made us, "... **forever perfect in the sight of God.**" As the Church together we have become the Ark of the New Covenant! We are vessels made to house His glory!

Let's go back, and look further at the scripture speaking of the promise we started this chapter with. But this time we'll use a New Testament reference from Hebrews.

"For if there had been nothing wrong with that first covenant, no place would have been sought for another. But God found fault with the people and said: "The time is coming, declares the Lord, when I will make a new covenant with the house of Israel and with the house of Judah. It will not be like the covenant I made with their forefathers when I took them by the hand to lead them out of Egypt, because they did not remain faithful to my covenant, and I turned away from them, declares the Lord.

This is the covenant I will make with the house of Israel after that time, declares the Lord. I will put my laws in their minds and write them on their hearts. I will be their God, and they will be my people. No longer will a man teach his neighbor, or a man his brother, saying, 'Know the Lord,' because they will all know me, from the least of them to the greatest. For I will forgive their wickedness and will remember their sins no more." By calling this covenant "new," he has made the first one obsolete; and what is obsolete and aging will soon disappear." (Hebrews 8:7-13)

Look at what the writer of Hebrews says was the reason for the ineffectiveness of the first covenant. In verse 8 it says, **"But God found fault with the people..."** There it is, we were not perfect, nor could we ever be on our own merit.

Not by our own works according to the law, nor by any sacrifices according to the law.

Galatians 2:16 says, **"...nevertheless knowing that a man is not justified by the works of the Law but through faith in Christ Jesus, even we have believed in Christ Jesus, that we may be justified by faith in Christ, and not by the works of the Law; since by the works of the Law <u>shall no flesh be justified</u>."**

The fault with the people was that they could not in the weakness of their flesh carry out the requirements of the law. And when they tried, it only brought more death to their conscience, because the law brought light to the fact that they still were like their forefather Adam, sinful. There were desires in them; that is in their flesh, which wanted the very things God said they shouldn't have.

Paul the Apostle spoke of the exposing of this Adam nature when he said in Romans 7:7-8, **"What shall we say then? Is the Law sin? May it never be! On the contrary, I would not have come to know what sin was except through the Law; for I would not have known about coveting if the Law had not said, "You shall not covet." But sin, taking opportunity through the commandment, produced in me coveting of every kind; for apart from the Law sin is dead (or unknown)."**

I realize the passage that this scripture is taken from in Romans, can be very confusing, but let me help you get the idea of just exactly what Paul is saying. You see the people were weak in obeying the law, because they were born from Adam's line, who himself was found to be unable to uphold the law, "Do not eat from this tree." Adam fell from being able to do what was good, because of his disobedience into sin.

17

Before the Law came to expose sin for what it really was, no one knew what it was, and therefore lived in it.

In the same way that doctor's need to discover the cause of a disease, in order to deal with a disease, so did through the Law the people discover their own disease of sin. And yes, through the Law, so have we all discovered our own sin. And now we can see that if sin followed the lineage of Adam through his seed, that seed could not have any part of the Holy sinless One it would take to establish a new Eternal covenant. Jesus had to be conceived by sinless seed. Otherwise He would have been born in sin, and thus been disqualified as the perfect sacrifice.

We discussed this earlier in the chapter. The main point I'm trying to make here, is that in and of ourselves, there was, and is, no ability whatsoever to restore fellowship with God. This was the purpose of the Law, to show us our own inadequacy, so we could look not to ourselves, but to Him alone for reconciliation. This is why we needed, a new and different way.

Isn't it interesting how the devil is working so hard nowadays to convince people that sin doesn't exist? You see this is what he does with the unbeliever; he veils their minds to the sin factor. **"And even if our gospel is veiled, it is veiled to those who are perishing, in whose case the god of this world has blinded the minds of the unbeliever, that they might not see the light of the gospel of the glory of Christ, who is the image of God." (2 Corinthians 4:3-4)**

However, the way they need to see the sin problem in their own lives now, is not only through the Law of sin and death, but in **"the light of the gospel of the glory of Christ."** You see there's a difference. Too many preachers are still trying to do the convicting of sin through preaching man-made religion and traditions. They try to condemn the sinner in showing them the error of their ways. Sinners already stand condemned, and it's the Holy Spirits' job to convict them of sin, not ours.

In the past, I've been guilty of this manipulative type of preaching myself. And you know what? You'll still get converts, just like the Pharisees did. And I won't get into what Jesus said about that. The problem is that these new believers will constantly struggle with a works based righteousness in their walk with God. I've seen it time and time again in my 25 years walking with the Lord. And until they hear about, and believe in, the Law of the Spirit of life in Christ through His love, there remains a guilt-ridden drive towards doing dead works. This is not at all the way we should walk out our faith. We must never forget why sinners were attracted to Jesus; because He loved them and forgave them! Shouldn't we follow His example?

Jesus didn't do anything He did out of fear, or guilt, or a striving to gain favor with God. He did the things He did out of His love for His Father, and His Father's love for Him. We therefore, should not be driven by anything but love. Jesus said, **"If you LOVE me you'll obey my commands."** Remember the old way wasn't working, we needed a new way. Jesus called this new way to be Born Again. Nicodemus was the first one even to hear about this new thing.

"Now there was a man of the Pharisees named Nicodemus, a member of the Jewish ruling council. He came to Jesus at night and said, "Rabbi, we know you are a teacher who has come from God.

19

For no one could perform the miraculous signs you are doing if God were not with him." In reply Jesus declared, "I tell you the truth, no one can see the kingdom of God unless he is born again."

"How can a man be born when he is old?" Nicodemus asked. "Surely he cannot enter a second time into his mother's womb to be born!"

Jesus answered, "I tell you the truth, no one can enter the kingdom of God unless he is born of water (women) and the Spirit (born again). Flesh gives birth to flesh, but the Spirit gives birth to spirit. You should not be surprised at my saying, <u>'You must be born again.'</u>

The wind blows wherever it pleases. You hear its sound, but you cannot tell where it comes from or where it is going. So it is with everyone born of the Spirit." (John 3:1-8)

Jesus said **NO ONE** can see the kingdom, unless he is Born Again. That 's a very exclusive statement to make, yet Jesus makes it loud and clear. So much for the Universalist who would have us believe that everyone gets in whether they want to or not. No Jesus says you MUST be Born Again. In other words, the old way is not working, it cannot get you where you need to go, it will not put you in the position you need to be in.

Simply put, the old vessel cannot carry what God wants you to carry in it, His Kingdom! God can be *among* the old vessel, but for Him to be *in* you, you need an upgrade! Even Jesus said you cannot put new wine into old wineskins; they will burst. That's why this new way, being Born Again, is so important to understand. Jesus made the way for us to be Born Again.

Without His sacrifice on the Cross to deal with Death and the Grave, we could not even be Born Again. Thus we could never see the Kingdom of God in us, and us in it!

1 Peter 1:23-24 says, "For you have been born again, not of perishable seed, but of imperishable, through the living and enduring word of God."

You see, the kingdom of God is Eternal. So the only way for us to live in it, and for it to live in us, is to be made alive eternally, to be Born Again!

The Kingdom of God will never perish, it is forever, the only way anyone could ever live in it, is if they are made alive eternally too.

Thank God! He made the way through Jesus Christ! We owe it all to Him!"**Praise be to the God and Father of our Lord Jesus Christ! In his great mercy he has given us new birth into a living hope through the resurrection of Jesus Christ from the dead, and into an inheritance that can never perish, spoil or fade — kept in heaven for you, who through faith are shielded by God's power until the coming of the salvation that is ready to be revealed in the last time." (1 Peter 1:3-6)**

Wow! We've been given a "New birth into a living hope!" This is an amazing truth to get a hold of folks! This is why the Bible says we are not like those in the world who are, "without God and without hope." All they have to live for, is an eventual, and inevitable death. But we have a living hope that goes beyond the grave, in Christ who went beyond the grave before us, as the scripture says, as the "first fruit from the dead." And to say there is a first, also means that there is a second, a third, a fourth and numbers more. As matter of fact, the Bible promises "As many shall call on the Name of the Lord" which is JESUS! Hallelujah what a promise!

CHAPTER TWO
Only One Way

**Jesus answered, "I am <u>the way</u> and the truth and the life.
No one comes to the Father except through me.**

John 14:6

Jesus the Promise came to show us the Way. We see in the New Testament, that His followers were called followers of the Way. The way of what you ask? The way to live with God in us, and us in Him through Christ. John the Beloved called it abiding. It is to live the same way as Jesus did, when He said, **"I and the Father are one."**

You see the power of His presence in us, is to help us become more like Christ. First and foremost in character, and then in both natural, and supernatural action. You see the character of Christ was and is ruled by love, hence how He fulfilled the Law. But love demands our action towards those who need it. We must remember however, action without love, whether natural or supernatural, does not impress God.

Paul the Apostle said in 1 Corinthians 13:1-3, **"If I speak in the tongues of men and of angels, but have not love, I am only a sounding gong or a clanging cymbal. If I have the gift of prophecy and can fathom all mysteries and all knowledge, and if I have a faith that can move mountains, but have not love, I am nothing. If I give all I possess to the poor and surrender my body to the flames, but have not love, I gain nothing."**

Then we also see Jesus saying in Matthew 7:21-23, "**Not everyone who says to me, 'Lord, Lord,' will enter the kingdom of heaven, but only he who does the will of my Father who is in heaven. Many will say to me on that day, 'Lord, Lord, did we not prophesy in your name and in your name drive out demons and perform many miracles?' Then I will tell them plainly, 'I never knew you. Away from me, you evildoers!'**

Those Jesus is referring to here, we're obviously not doing the will of the Father. Because He bases His judgment against them with the words, **"…only he who does the will of my Father who is in heaven."** When Jesus was asked what the will of the Father was by the disciples, he didn't respond, "Love signs and wonders with all your heart, soul, mind and strength." He said, "Love the Lord with all your heart…" And secondly He never said, "Love your gifts as much as yourself." Are you getting the point? **"And now these three remain: faith, hope and love. But the greatest of these is love." (1 Corinthians 13:13)** And the in 1 Corinthians 14:11 it says, **"Follow the way of love and eagerly desire spiritual gifts, especially the gift of prophecy."**It does not say follow the way of spiritual gifts and desire love. We must first "be" before we can "do".

Remember, they were first called Christians (little Christ's) in Antioch, because they were recognized as being like Christ, saying and doing the things He did.

Those previously mentioned in Matthew 7:21-23, wrongly put the cart before the horse. I am reminded of the Seven Sons of Sceva as a perfect example of what we're referring to here.

"Some Jews who went around driving out evil spirits tried to invoke the name of the Lord Jesus over those who were demon-possessed. They would say, "In the name of Jesus, whom Paul preaches, I command you to come out." Seven sons of Sceva, a Jewish chief priest, were doing this. [One day] the evil spirit answered them, "Jesus I know, and I know about Paul, but who are you?" Then the man who had the evil spirit jumped on them and overpowered them all. He gave them such a beating that they ran out of the house naked and bleeding." (Acts 19:13-16)

You see, they got the "do" before the "be". Note, the demons knew Paul. When you, like Paul, allow the power God has vested in you to form Christ in you, the demons will know and listen to you. Not because of you directly, but "...because the one who is in you is greater than the one who is in the world." (1 John 4:4) They knew Paul, because it was no longer him that lived, but Christ who lived in him. (Galatians 2:20) Paul was walking in the Way, that of Christ, the anointed life.

Let me share a personal example. When I was still Youth Pastoring a number of years ago, we were holding a Youth Conference at our Church one weekend. As the worship band began moving into spiritual songs to God, a young girl began to manifest in an ungodly manner on the floor. You see, that's what happens when Jesus show's up. It did in the Bible, and it still does today. It was obvious this was not God and my leader's who were present got that twist on the inside too. This was not the Holy Spirit! So being that I was the Youth Pastor hosting the event, they all looked to me for guidance.

Even the guest speaker, who was ministering in the prayer line tapped me on the shoulder on the way by and said, "This one is yours buddy." I still don't know if he meant

"Yours" as in she was in my Youth Group or "Yours" as in handling the present sticky situation.

Anyways, walking towards the scene, I began saying out loud, "I have Christ in me the hope of Glory, therefore it is no longer I that live, but Christ who lives in me. Greater is He who is in me, than he that is in the world." I no sooner finished saying this when; it literally felt like electricity exploding forth in the core of my being (my inner man). It was unrecognized by my five natural senses; but I quickly discerned it to be supernatural.

I knew in that moment, that I was experiencing a release of the power that God had vested in me from within!! I quickly told the female leader's around her, to get her to her feet. I spoke her name to make sure I had her attention first, and not the spirits'. And I then asked her, "Do you want to be free of this?" She said, "Yes." And no sooner did she say yes, that I said, "In the name of Jesus Christ of Nazareth, you unclean spirit come out!!" Well I tell you, so much power went through me into her that she and I and everyone around us were nearly knocked over. And Hallelujah!! She was set free!! She received Christ and was filled with the Holy Spirit after this.

That's what the anointing is for, to set free those held captive to the devil! It's to crush the yoke of bondage! Put it this way, if I can be frank, that demon had no hope in hell, for if God is for me, who can stand against me! You may think this sounds overconfident. Listen, you cannot overextend your confidence in Jesus Christ! He is the King of Kings, the Lord of Lords, at the very mention of His glorious Name, all Hell shakes in fear!

I believe fear is the currency of Hell; it's what they bank on every day, with every person they are trying to intimidate.

However, the Bible clearly states that, **"We have not been given a spirit of fear..."** It's not how God operates! The only place we are in danger of placing our confidence, is in our flesh. However, even though this was a powerful experience in my life, I rejoice not in the fact that the demonic spirit was subject to Christ in me, but that a young woman was freed from an area of bondage to Satan. You see this is the Way of Christ. This is the anointing that crushes every yoke of bondage!

Love ALWAYS needs to be our motive for the use of His power and authority from the source of His incredible Presence in us!

THE WAY CONTINUED

"The Holy Spirit was showing by this that the way into the Most Holy Place had not yet been disclosed as long as the first tabernacle was still standing." (Hebrews 9:8)

Jesus answered, "I am the way and the truth and the life. No one comes to the Father except through me. (John 14:6)

The Holy Spirit also testifies to us about this. First he says: "This is the covenant I will make with them after that time, says the Lord. I will put my laws in their hearts, and I will write them on their minds." Then he adds: "Their sins and lawless acts I will remember no more." And where these have been forgiven, there is no longer any sacrifice for sin.

Therefore, brothers, since we have confidence to enter the Most Holy Place by the blood of Jesus, by a new and living way opened for us through the curtain, that is, his body, and since we have a great priest over the house of God, let us draw near to God with a sincere heart in full assurance of faith, having our hearts sprinkled to cleanse us from a guilty conscience and having our bodies washed with pure water. (Hebrews 10:15-22)

Then he said, "Here I am, I have come to do your will." He sets aside the first to establish the second. And by that will, we have been made holy through the sacrifice of the body of Jesus Christ once for all. (Hebrews 10:9-10)

Are you getting it? Do you see it? Hallelujah, He did it! For the Lord could not dwell in the presence of sin, so in order for Him to dwell in us as His temple, we had to be cleansed from sin. *"...having our hearts sprinkled to cleanse us from a guilty conscience and having our bodies washed with pure water."* "For God made Him who knew no sin to become sin on our behalf that we might become the righteousness of God in Him." (2 Corinthians 5:21)

It's so clear... it jumps right out at you. Jesus made the way for us to become vessels worthy of housing His presence through the Holy Spirit. It's semantics perhaps, but we don't need to go into the Holy of Holies, because the Holy of Holies through Jesus has gone into us! Wow! How does this change your perspective on being a Christian? We have constant access to the temple...because we are one! "Do you not know that you are a temple of God, and that the Spirit of God dwells in you? (1 Corinthians 3:16-17) When we sin, we don't have to travel to the nearest temple to see the priest.

"If we confess our sins, He is faithful and righteous to forgive us our sins and to cleanse us from all unrighteousness." (1 John 1:9) ...right now, wherever we are!

"My little children, I am writing these things to you that you may not sin. And if anyone sins, <u>we have</u> an <u>Advocate</u> with the Father, Jesus Christ the righteous; and He Himself is the propitiation for our sins; and not for ours only, but also for those of the whole world. (1 John 2:1-3)

You see, Jesus made the way, by becoming the Way. To show this I want to take a closer look at one of the verses I used to start this section. Hebrews 9:8 says, **"The Holy Spirit was showing by this that the way into the Most Holy Place had not yet been disclosed <u>as long as the first tabernacle was still standing."</u>**

In other words the first had to fall in order for the second to be built. So when specifically was the first tabernacle torn down then to make way for the second? And wasn't there more than just one tabernacle in Jerusalem. Were all the tabernacles in Jerusalem to be torn down? Obviously the author of Hebrews had to be referring to one type of tabernacle being replaced by another type.

In John 2:18-20, **"The Jews therefore answered and said to Him, "What sign do You show to us, seeing that You do these things?" Jesus answered and said to them, "Destroy this temple, and in three days I will raise it up."** Jesus' pre-resurrection body represented the old temple or tabernacle, because He came in it to earth under the Law. But at the point of His physical death on the cross, the old temple and its temporary ways of ceremonial cleansing from sin were destroyed with Him. The author of Hebrews goes into this in much detail.

Hebrews 9:12-14 says, **"He did not enter by means of the blood of goats and calves; but he entered the Most Holy Place once for all by his own blood, having obtained eternal redemption. The blood of goats and bulls and the ashes of a heifer sprinkled on those who are ceremonially unclean sanctify them so that they are outwardly clean. How much more, then, will the blood of Christ, who through the eternal Spirit offered himself unblemished to God, cleanse our consciences from acts that lead to death, so that we may serve the living God?"**

Praise the Lord! We no longer have temporary cleansing from sin and death; but eternal and ongoing cleansing. We also hear of the temple veil actually being ripped from top to bottom at the very time of Christ's death. This signifying of course, that the old way of doing it was done! Hallelujah it is finished!!

After Christ rose from the dead, He met with his disciples. And among other things, he showed them His new temple. His new body, a temple. And that now they too could have access to the Holy of Holies being in them, by believing in Him and being saved! **"Here I am! I stand at the door and knock. If anyone hears my voice and opens the door, <u>I will come in</u> and eat with him, and he with me." (Revelation 3:20)**

Through Jesus Christ there has a way been made. **"And this is the testimony: God has given us eternal life, and this life is in his Son. He who has the Son has life; he who does not have the Son of God does not have life." (1 John 5:11-12)**

"For this reason Christ is the mediator of a new covenant, that those who call on Him may receive the promised eternal inheritance, now that He has died as a ransom to

set them free from the sins committed under the first covenant." (Hebrews 9:15)

"And it shall be, that everyone who calls on the name of the Lord shall be saved.' (Acts 2:21)

"Consequently, just as the result of one trespass was condemnation for all men, so also the result of one act of righteousness was justification that brings life for all men. For just as through the disobedience of the one man the many were made sinners, so also through the obedience of the one.

The law was added so that the trespass might increase. But where sin increased, grace increased all the more, so that, just as sin reigned in death, so also grace might reign through righteousness to bring eternal life through Jesus Christ our Lord." (Romans 5:18-21)

I thank Jesus for becoming the way to a better covenant. Because of Him, we are able to experience what the prophets of old could only long to see. I am now the righteousness of God Himself, in and through Christ! So the Power of God's Presence can now dwell in me! "I had to become as righteous as You are Father in order for You to live in me." And Christ has made a way for You to live in me. I now stand "not guilty" before the courts of heaven, as a new man without sin, spot or blemish. For I have Christ "the anointed One" in me, the hope of glory!!

Jesus said at one point, that the time had come for him to return to his glory in heaven, but before this He said, "I must fall and die like a kernel of wheat that falls into the furrows of the earth. Unless I die I will be alone-a single seed. But my death will produce many new wheat kernels-a plentiful harvest of new lives. (John 12:23)

OUR POSITION IN HIM

The Bible is incredibly clear that we are positioned with Christ. So that begs the question where is Christ now? Ephesians 1:18-21 says, **"I pray also that the eyes of your heart may be enlightened in order that you may <u>know the hope</u> to which he has called you, the riches of his glorious inheritance in the saints, and his <u>incomparably great power for us who believe</u>.**

That power is like the working of his mighty strength, which he exerted in Christ when <u>God raised him from the dead and seated him at his right hand in the heavenly realms</u>, far above all rule and authority, power and dominion, and every title that can be given, not only in the present age but also in the one to come."

So where is Christ? **"God raised him from the dead and seated him <u>at his right hand</u> in the heavenly realms…"** So where does that place you, if you are indeed seated with Christ? Scriptural logic and reasoning should lead you to the same amazing conclusion I've come to. Those who are in Christ, because He is in them, are seated with Jesus at the right hand of God!!

Ephesians 2:4-84 says, **"But because of his great love for us, God, who is rich in mercy, made us alive with Christ even when we were dead in transgressions — it is by grace you have been saved. And God raised us up with Christ and <u>seated us with him in the heavenly realms</u> in Christ Jesus, in order that in the coming ages he might show the incomparable riches of his grace, expressed in his kindness to us in Christ Jesus."**

You might be thinking to yourself, "Well I don't feel like I'm seated there." Listen folks, this is a spiritual truth and reality, you can't feel it, you faith it! It can only be appropriated in your life by faith in what Jesus has done, and how He has positioned you in Him. We need to understand this, it's essential in allowing the power of His presence to flow out of your temple, that very treasure stored in your earthly vessel. The power of God in the Name of Jesus, and your position and possession in that name and person of Christ!

Peter said to the lame beggar at the Temple gate, **"Gold and Silver I do not <u>possess</u>, but what I do <u>possess</u>, I give to you. In the <u>name</u> of Jesus Christ of Nazareth get up and walk!"** You see, one can operate in authority only when they know that they've been given authority. Peter knew His POSITION in and POSSESSION of Christ's name, and ministered out of them. As believers, we must minister in the same manner that has been laid out for us by Jesus and all who followed Him. Out of POSITION and POSSESSION.

Position being where God has placed me in Jesus through what He did on the cross, and how my belief in that causes me to be positioned far differently than I was prior to believing. And possession, being what I now have, because of the position God has placed me in Christ! This is why the teaching of who we are in Christ is so important. You can't use what you don't even know you have. The New Testament is full of amazing truths of who we are, and what we have in Christ Jesus!

Only the sons get an inheritance, the servants do not.

It's time the people of God start walking as sons and not servants! This does not mean we don't serve God, on the contrary it means we now serve out of sonship!

Have you noticed the medias' recent onslaught against Jesus being the Only Way? It's become a huge issue even in circles of secular society. The topic has even been discussed on Oprah. And no wonder; the devil knows about the rich treasures available in Christ, and he wants to make sure no one gets them, period!

An individual, void of Christ, is no threat to the Devil and His crumbling Kingdom. However to have Christ in you, is greater than he that is in the world, that is the Devil. We exist as the Church to carry on the work that Jesus did while manifest in flesh on the Earth. What was His work? **"For this purpose the Son of God was manifested, that He might destroy the works of the devil."** (1 John 3:8-9) And **"God anointed Jesus of Nazareth with the Holy Spirit and power, and he went around doing good and healing all who were under the power of the devil, because God was with him."(Acts 10:38)** Do you think the Devil wants us carrying on this work? NO. This is why he attacks the Way. This is why he causes the world to doubt the Way. This is why he works hard to maintain "the wide road" that leads to destruction, to distract the world from the narrow path; the Way that leads to life.

THE NEW VEHICLE

"But we have this treasure in earthen vessels, so that the surpassing greatness of the power may be of God and not from ourselves." (2 Corinthians 4:7)

"Do you not know that your body is a temple of the Holy Spirit, who is in you, whom you have received from God? You are not your own; you were bought at a price. Therefore honor God with your body. (1 Corinthians 6:19-20)

You know, I love how Jesus dropped hints all the time about what He was up to. For instance He revealed the plan of our bodies' purpose to become the temple of God when He said, **"Tear down this temple (speaking of His body) and I will raise it up again in three days."** And of course it was misunderstood and went right over people's heads as usual. Jesus was revealing that He would make a way for us to have God inhabit His people, that He would make us **"a temple not made with hands."**

You know, whether you realize it or not, your Mom and Dad didn't make you... God did! I never knit my now 9 year old son Judah together in Patricia's womb... God did! He was not made with human hands. Scientist's and Medical Society alike are still baffled and do not fully understand how it all works! You my friend, have not been made with human hands, so this therefore qualifies you to be a potential Temple of the God of the Universe! And by potential I mean you still have ask Him into your life if you haven't already.

Why don't you go ahead right now and become a Temple of His Presence, call on the Name of Lord Jesus and be saved! Yeah, it is that simple, and yet that amazing!

I absolutely adore God's wisdom and how He is working out His plan. I mean He has put His unsurpassing power and strength into absolutely weak and fault prone vessels; you and I. He always works at confounding the wise by using the weak. What wise investor invests all of his resources into a failing commodity? Yet this is exactly what God did. He invested all He had in us.

Have you ever really taken a good look at the disciples Jesus picked at the Father's direction? Man, I look at them and think, "If God can use those bumbling fools, then He can use this one!" If you were Jesus would you have picked them? Or would you have picked those with the PhD's and BA's of that day? And by the way that would have been the Pharisees and Sadducees....hmmm.

And no I am not at all against study and scholastic accomplishments, but it should be study for transformation of our hearts, not just information to fill our heads. God knows we have enough information, we're fat with it!!

When the Pharisees saw the disciples after the resurrection and ascension of Jesus, they were saying and doing the things Jesus did. And they wondered how they knew the Law and the Prophets as well as they did. Yet they had never been through the regular hoops of traditional training! It was simply a practical display, by believers of a New Covenant life! **This is the covenant I will make with the house of Israel after that time, declares the Lord.**

"I will put my laws in their minds and write them on their hearts. I will be their God, and they will be my people. <u>No longer will a man need to teach his neighbor</u>, or a man his brother, saying, 'Know the Lord,' because they will all know me, from the least of them to the greatest. For I will forgive their wickedness and will remember their sins no more." By calling this covenant "new," he has made the first one obsolete; and what is obsolete and aging will soon disappear." (Hebrews 8:10-9:1)

And...

As for you, the anointing you received from him remains in you, and <u>you do not need anyone to teach you</u>. But as <u>his anointing teaches you about all things</u> and as that anointing is real, not counterfeit — just as it has taught you, remain in him. (1 John 2:27) This by the way does not mean that the office of teacher needs to be thrown out of the Church. I for one hope that's not the case; I love to teach! The Apostle Paul is very clear that God has given some the gift of teaching. But it means to teach the logos (that which has been physically recorded) not that which is written on the heart. What is written on the heart is called revelation. It's when what is being taught, suddenly gets caught! Only the Holy Spirit can do this. A perfect example is when Jesus asked Simon Peter, **"Who do you say that I am?"** And Peter answered, **"You are the Christ, the Messiah, the Son of the Living God!"** Jesus then says to Him, **"I tell you the truth; flesh and blood did not reveal this to you, but my Father in Heaven."**

In other words Jesus was saying, "Peter you weren't taught this, you caught it!" You see what has only been taught to us, can easily be taken away or changed when someone who is better at teaching comes along. However, what you have caught can never be taken away, not even by the greatest teacher! Conveying the information is the teacher's responsibility, receiving it into your heart is your "response - ability" and making it alive in you is God's ability! Experiencing revelation concerning God and His Kingdom through His word and how it applies to you, is what builds "the word of your testimony."

Remember John's revelation in Chapter 12 when he saw the vision of Satan being cast down? It speaks of how the people of God overcame him... **"...by the blood of the Lamb and the word of their testimony."** What was the word of their testimony? Jesus and their REVELATION of Him in them as the Christ, the Anointed One, and all He had done for them.

THE MYSTERY REVEALED

Colossians 1:25-27 says...**"I have become its (the Church) servant by the commission God gave me to present to you the word of God in its fullness—the mystery that has been** kept hidden for ages and generations, but is now disclosed to the saints. And to them God has chosen to make known among the Gentiles the glorious riches of this mystery, **which is** Christ in you, the hope of glory."

That's it!! God's secret plan hidden in prophetic utterance for ages has now been revealed to us!! No wonder the prophets of old long to see our days! God planned all along to go from being God among us, to God living within us through His Spirit! And of course, how else could we truly incarnate Christ to the world if God wasn't in us? I mean talk about having purpose in life....Wow!

We have been called to carry the Presence of Our Almighty God in these weak bodies; and **"Not by might, not strength, but by my Spirit says the Lord."** (Zechariah 4:6) In Roman 8:10-11 it says... **"And if Christ is in you, the body is dead because of sin, but the Spirit is alive (reborn) because of righteousness. But if the Spirit of Him who raised Jesus from the dead dwells in you, He who raised Christ from the dead will also give life to your mortal bodies through His Spirit who dwells in you."** Did you hear that! If you're a believer, the Spirit of God who raised Jesus from the dead lives in you!!

You have resurrection life and power inside of you!! Jesus said, **"I am the resurrection and the life."** If you opened the door and invited Jesus in when He came knocking, you now have in you "the Resurrection" and "the Life"!

We now know for ourselves personally that we have life, but what about letting that life and resurrection flow out of us to others who need Jesus? Just imagine what could happen. Remember Peter and John at the temple? They said, **"What we have (or possess) we give you."** What did they have?

Life and Resurrection power in the Name of Jesus! Jesus was very clear in the scriptures, that He came to give us life more abundantly. In greater measure than we could ever experience apart from Him.

"Do you not know that your body is a temple of the Spirit of God, who is in you, whom you have received from God?" (2 Corinthians 6:19)

In the scriptures "the heart" and "the spirit" are mainly viewed in synonymous terms. And this is most likely because they both refer to the deepest core of our being. So in view of this, when God put His own Spirit in us, He literally put His heart in us. We were all in dire need of a heart transplant, **"The heart is deceitful above all things, and it is exceedingly corrupt..."(Jeremiah 17:9)**

God answered the clarion call of the fallen human race for a new heart! And He showed us by sending and giving up Jesus on the cross, His only Son, not one of many, His only Son. And He did this because He loved us! Jesus was and is the fullest expression of God giving us His heart. And His heart was and is for us... people. That's why the second command after loving God is to love others.

If you truly love God and come to know His heart, you will love others, because God's heart is for people. The scriptures are very clear that if you say you love God yet hate your brother, you've got it all wrong. So it's simple: If you love God, you'll love people. The more you fall in love with your Heavenly Father, the more you'll love people.

LOVE DEMANDS ACTION

We have to understand this, "For God so loved the world that He GAVE..." When we truly love something or someone, it moves us to action! And most times it happens effortlessly because true love always produces action. The band Boston hit the nail on the head when they said that love is "More than a Feeling". Sorry, I'm an 80's child at heart when it comes to my musical preference; even my Church teases me about it.

Just so we're keeping on task here, I'm pointing out love as a motivator for a reason. We have seen thus far that God has created us to be vehicles of His presence. Just as much as gasoline is needed to help vehicles to get many places, not to stay in one place.

Love is the fuel for our vessel to go many places not just to stay in one. Jesus said, "As I have loved you, love one another." In other words, God fills us with His love not just for us, but to pour out and into others. Jesus didn't exclusively minister the love and power of God in the Temple; in fact He did it there the least. Jesus modeled for us how to be a temple of God in everyday life, everywhere He went! The Pharisee's tried to make access to the Presence of God hard and burdensome, and only for the select few. Meanwhile Jesus took the Kingdom of God to the place the Pharisee's thought blasphemous even to mention, the place of sinners.

You see, Jesus never told the disciples to wait and receive the baptism of the Holy Spirit so they could keep the power to themselves and a select few. Remember that's what the Pharisee's did with the Law. God gave us His Spirit for power to be witnesses. Notice it says "to be" witnesses. We are to literally "become" witnesses not just "do" some witnessing. Witnessing is a 24/7 lifestyle, not a onetime event! And the Great Commission which is for "all who believe" not "some who may be called" commands us to GO! Not to stay!

Over the years, I've heard so many people ask the question, "Where has the power of the Church gone?" The truth is; it hasn't gone anywhere. And that's the problem.

It's sitting in the pew next to you in Church buildings all over North America! Wait a minute; it's sitting in the very seat you're sitting in! Getting the point? The Gospel is "the Power of God unto salvation". And God displays that power the greatest, when we take it to those who need it. And the majority of those people will not be found in a Church facility.

I'm not saying we're to go out and jam biblical information down people's throats, there's enough of that going on with little, to no effect. Neither am I saying let's not mention Jesus name lest we offend someone. What I am saying is the Church in general needs to stop living a double life, warm enough to fit in with the hot, and cool enough to fit in with the cold. That's called "lukewarm" remember the warning from God to those who are lukewarm? It's not good... not good at all. However, when you're in love with someone, you can't stop talking about them, thinking about them and about what you want to do for them. It's no different with Jesus.

In this state of love, whenever you share with someone else about your love interest, it's always with a genuine passion. This genuine passion can be so strong in fact, that it causes those that hear you to either get annoyed, or to desire to have the same love you do. Obviously we hope for the latter, but I have had people get annoyed when I talk about my love for Jesus. But have you ever noticed that just because people get annoyed, it never silences the one who is in love?

Though it may appear to be the case in our information driven culture, people are not really looking for more information. They are looking for someone who lives in a way that is genuine and backed up by the things they do, not only in what they say. Neither Jesus, nor the disciples said anything, without also backing it up with what they did. I believe the world is more tired of a Church that never demonstrates it claims, than the Church itself is.

Church we have no excuse; God has given us the vehicle, the fuel, and the map. We must therefore "GO"! You may be fighting the thought, "Well I'm not worthy." Well join the club, none of us are, which is exactly why He chose us and made us worthy in Christ! So get over yourself and get out to others! Listen, if God didn't think you were worth anything; then He wouldn't have spent the life of His Son on you! Yet the fact remains that He completed the transaction!

He's invested everything He has into people; you and I. Simply because to Him we were worth it!

It never ceases to amaze me that God invested everything He had into a failed commodity! How many wise investors would do that! Thank God He operates by a different wisdom!

CONTENTS OF THE NEW VESSEL

In the first chapter we discussed the contents found in the Old Ark. If the theme of this book holds true, that we have become the new vessel carrying the Presence of God, then you would think that you would find some correlation between the two? Well you're right and here are the correlations. The first item placed in the old Ark was the Word of Testimony or Ten Commandments. The Testimony was the first and foremost item placed in the ark. In this New Covenant it has also first and foremost been placed in us. Remember Hebrews 8:10 says, **"This is the covenant I will make with the house of Israel after that time, declares the Lord. I will <u>put my laws in their minds</u> and <u>write them</u>**

<u>on their hearts.</u> **I will be their God, and they will be my people."** Like the old ark, we contain the Testimony!

The next item placed in the Ark was a measure of the Manna from heaven. It was placed before the Testimony so the Testimony would preserve it. I find this particularly interesting considering the scriptures speak of the Word of God preserving, and holding all things together. Jesus was very clear regarding Himself being the true bread. In John 6:32-36 Jesus said to them, **"I tell you the truth, it is not Moses who has given you the bread from heaven, but it is my Father who gives you the true bread from heaven. The bread of God is he who comes down from heaven, and gives life to the world." "Sir," they said, "from now on give us this bread." Then Jesus declared, "I am the bread of life. He who comes to me will never go hungry, and he who believes in me will never be thirsty."** And later on He says in verse 51, **"This is the bread that came down from heaven. Your forefathers ate manna and died, but he who feeds on this bread will live forever."** When we receive Jesus into our heart and life, we have in this manner, consumed true bread from Heaven.

The last item placed in the Ark, was Aaron's staff that budded when placed overnight in the Tent of Meeting. Remember, the one staff that budded out of the 12 staffs of the tribes of Israel identified the Tribe to be named God's chosen priesthood. Well, in 1 Peter 2:9 it says regarding us under the New Covenant , **"But you are a <u>chosen people,</u> a <u>royal priesthood,</u> a holy nation, a people belonging to God, that you may declare the praises of him who called you out of darkness into his wonderful light."**

Those who choose to receive Jesus Christ, have become a chosen people and a royal priesthood onto God!

That's it, all three contents found in the Old Ark of the Old Covenant, have been carried over into the New Covenant and its Ark, the people of God, His Church! Folks I don't know about you, but this to me is astounding! Remember what amazing miracles and events surrounded the old Ark? Yet the writer of Hebrews tells us in Hebrews 8:6 that, **"...we have a better covenant established on better promises."**

Haggai tells us concerning this covenant in Chapter 2 verse 9 that... **"The glory of this latter <u>house</u> (dwelling) shall be greater than that of the former, says the Lord of hosts."** And then in 2 Corinthians 3:18 it tells us that this presence of God will be so great, it will transform us into the very likeness of God Himself! **"And we, who with unveiled faces all reflect the Lord's glory, are being transformed into his likeness with ever-increasing glory, which comes from the Lord, who is the Spirit."**

A SINGLE BOX OR MANY PEOPLE

If you think about it, which do you think is more effective in displaying and spreading the power of God? A single box, carried by a select few, and limited by location? Or the millions of people who have received Jesus into their hearts and lives over the past thousands of years. Who also go to work every day, travel everywhere, and meet hundreds of people over their life time? To me it's a "no-brainer". And once again we see that this was God's amazing plan from the get go.

Jesus reveals this in John 12:24-25 when He said, **"I tell you the truth, unless a kernel of wheat falls to the ground and dies, it remains only a single seed. But if it dies, it produces <u>many</u> seeds."** In Hebrews 2:10 it says that Jesus death was responsible for, **"...bringing <u>many</u> sons to glory."**

Our mission is very clear; it is to allow the Presence of God in us, to flow out and into everyday life wherever we go, and in whatever we do. What this world is looking for is the Power to Change. And nothing can bring change in a person's life, like the Power of the Presence of God!

There are no substitutes for the Kingdom of God invading your life.

The world has lots to offer, but nothing ever comes close to the righteousness, peace, and joy found in the Presence. Moses knew this, when the Lord offered to have an Angel lead the Israelites into the promised land, Moses refuted that option saying, **"Unless Your Presence goes with us we will not leave here."** And by the way, the "here" he was referring to, was the desert. Still, Moses wasn't even slightly tempted by the offer of accompaniment by a mighty Angel into the Promised Land. I mean think about it, it's recorded in scripture how one angel took out thousands of warriors without breaking a sweat! But no, Moses didn't even think twice! Why? He knew the Presence. Once you get a taste of the Presence of God, everything else pales in comparison. Like the words to that old song, "Turn your eyes upon Jesus. Look full in His wonderful face and the things of this Earth will grow strangely dim…"

Once you taste and see, you know that God is good! And you now see that the other things you used to seek, weren't really that good after all. However we must remember that God chooses to only be found by those who are seeking Him. Whether they know it not, if they're seeking truth, they will come to God. Unfortunately many, including some in the Church today, could care less about taking the time to seek God. Nevertheless, His promise remains that, **"He rewards those who diligently seek Him."** (Hebrews 11:6)

For the past couple of weeks the Lord has led my studies into the Books of Kings. One of the main themes expressed and recorded in these historical accounts is that God rewards those who seek Him. Every king that ruled in Israel and Judah that, "Inquired of the Lord" prospered greatly, conquered every enemy, and lived out their days in peace and health. I do not think for one minute that this principle has ever changed.

So if you're wondering why your life is a wreck, your health and finances are deteriorating, and you can't seem to find any peace, let me ask you, have you inquired of God lately? I've learned in my Christian walk, that the only one that can stop me from seeking God, is me. I cannot blame anyone else, even the devil.

A Pastor friend of mine once said; that one of his personal goals in his relationship with Jesus, is to get to know Him so well in the here and now, that when He appears in the sky he would already recognize Him! You think that's too lofty a goal? Maybe, but it's a good one. I think our goals should be a lot loftier as a Church, than they have been in the past. Let's not forget that our, **"God is able to do immeasurably more than all we ask or imagine, according to <u>his power</u> that is at work <u>within us</u>..." (Ephesians 3:20)**

CHAPTER 3
A Manual and Demonstration

I tell you the truth, anyone who has faith in me <u>will do what I have been doing</u>. He will do even greater things than these, because I am going to the Father.

John 14:12

This is how we know we are in him: Whoever claims to live in him <u>must </u>walk in the same manner as <u>Jesus did</u>.

1 John 2:5-6

I'm continually amazed at how Bible scholars either ignore, or try to contextualize the meaning out of the above passages! My wife and I decided years ago to take Jesus at His word. Aside from parables, and illustrative statements with symbolic meaning, which are up for interpretation, we take what He has told us to do literally. When He says that if I have faith I can do what He did, I believe it! When He says he will do whatever I ask in His name, I believe it!

And then John tells me that if I claim to know Jesus, I should also walk as He did. I take this literally! I'm tired of cessationalist theology disempowering the Church! If you're not familiar with cessationalism, it's the view that the charismatic gifts of the Holy Spirit, such as tongues, prophecy and healing, ceased being practiced early on in Church history.

This is complete foolishness, rooted in unbelief and supported with a few select "out of context" scriptures. However, just so I'm being fair to both sides of the argument, here's the major proof text that is supposedly supporting a present absence of the gifts. 1 Corinthians 13:8-10 says, **"Love never fails. But where there are prophecies, they will cease; where there are tongues, they will be stilled; where there is knowledge, it will pass away. For we know in part and we prophesy in part, but when that which is perfect comes, that which is imperfect will disappear."**

Cessationalist's believe that since we now have the finished canonized Bible, that "it "indeed is the perfection that has appeared. And by the way, I believe in the inerrancy of scripture, just so we're clear. But in keeping with their logic this scripture would be saying that the gifts are not needed anymore. And that imperfection itself has also disappeared! The last time I looked there remains much imperfection all around us! The problem lies first in the interpretation of **"that which is perfect."**

I believe scripture more strongly supports, **"that which is perfect"** to be the Kingdom of Heaven come to earth! When the kingdom comes, there will be no more imperfection period! No more tears, death, sorrow, sin. In the kingdom we'll have no need for tongues and interpretation, prophecy and word of knowledge, healing and miracles. And that's because "that which is perfect" will be here on Earth. No one will be sick, so they'll be no need for healing. All that is imperfect will disappear, because imperfection has no place in the Kingdom of God! God is perfect! And He has made us to be able to dwell in this perfect Kingdom by perfecting us in Christ! In view of God's mandate to restore His kingdom, a kingdom interpretation of this passage is a far more scripturally sensible interpretation.

2 Peter 3:13 says, **"But in keeping with his promise we are looking forward to a new heaven and a new earth, the home of righteousness."** Righteousness here in regards to the kingdom of God means: just, complete, and perfect. It will be where perfection dwells, and all who dwell in it will be perfect! The Bride will then have no spots or wrinkles; she will have been perfected in this age for the one to come, the Kingdom!

I believe everything Jesus did; He did first to obey the Father, and second as an example for us to follow. An example of how we too can walk in the power of God, full of the Holy Spirit! That's why He said, **"I must go, so He (the Spirit) can come to you."** And, **"Go wait in Jerusalem for the promise of the Father."** What was the promise? That God would give us His heart, His very own Spirit who was on and in Jesus during His earthly ministry.

Jesus would never justly give us a command without providing the tools for us to fulfill that command.

If you think about it, much of the records of Jesus life in the New Testament, are of Him doing miracles. Remember He said in John 14:12, **"<u>Anyone</u> who has faith in Me, will do what I have been doing."** Well what had Jesus been doing up to that point? He had cast out demons, raised the dead, healed the sick, and opened the eyes of the blind to name a few. And again I remind you, Jesus said, **"Anyone who has faith in Me, will do what I have been doing."** Notice He said, **"Anyone"**? He never said only someone! And the only requirement is that we have faith in Him.

So let's make sure we're clear on this. If you have faith in Jesus, Jesus said you WILL DO the things that HE DID! When Jesus came to the boat walking on the water, Peter asked, **"Lord if it is you, tell me to come to you."**

I love this, Jesus said, **"Come!"** Jesus never laid out for Peter an eloquently prepared thesis on why Peter couldn't really walk on water, and then preached it to him. No, He just said, "Come!" And then Peter did what Jesus was doing by faith in Jesus. And remember, he never began to sink, until he began to doubt. So what's the point here? You will never be able to do the things Jesus did if you do not have faith in Him. Peter is often criticized in messages and sermons. But I say, at least he got out of the boat and tried! That's more than most folks are doing for Jesus.

Of course it doesn't help when we have modern-day "teachers of the law" telling us that we can't do it because God's power has somehow evacuated the premises! All this based on the unbelief in their hearts! It doesn't sound a whole lot different than it did in Jesus day, does it? We must not forget the demonstrative part of the Great Commission.

In Mark 16:17-18 Jesus promises us that these things will accompany the preaching of the word. He said, **"And these signs will follow those who believe in My name: they will cast out demons; they will speak with new tongues; they will take up serpents; and if they drink anything deadly, it will by no means hurt them; they will lay hands on the sick, and they will recover."**

If the cessationalists are right, then somewhere along the way the last half of the Great Commission fell off the wagon. It also means that whether you believe in the Name of Jesus or not, the power is just not there for you anymore, so sorry. Folks this just doesn't hold water in my experience, and I find it to be scripturally ridiculous! Peter and Johns' response to all those in the Temple thinking that they healed the lame man by their own power was this, **"This man stands before healed because of _faith in the Name_ of the Lord Jesus Christ!"**

Whose faith? Not the lame beggars', he just wanted money. It was Peter and Johns' faith and reliance on the Power of the Name of Jesus! Although, the beggar was definitely expecting to receive something too, and he did indeed! Far more than he bargained for! They gave him what they had, faith in that whatever they asked, Jesus would do!

People of God, we've been given a manual, (the Bible) with plenty of examples of Jesus doing the very same things He has now asked us to do in His Name. We are accountable to preach the Gospel of salvation to all creation, cast out devils, heal the sick, and yes even raise the dead! And walking in the same manner that Jesus did, gives us confidence that we are indeed in him. Remember 1 John 2:5 – 6? **"This is how we know we are in him: Whoever claims to live in him must walk in the same manner as <u>Jesus did</u>."**

You need to see God's wisdom in this, when Jesus was manifest in the flesh during His earthly ministry, He limited himself to that flesh. And by this I mean, He could only be in one place, at one time, with only those people within His reach. But now Jesus can be Himself through anyone of us, at any time, in any place, to anyone, if only we would just let Him.

EQUIPPED AND SUPPLIED

"His <u>divine power</u> has given us <u>everything we need</u> for life and godliness through our knowledge of him who called us by his own glory and goodness." (2 Peter 1:3-4)

You see, God has given us every tool we need to get the job done, but it's up to us to step out of the boat and use those tools. It's up to you to rise above what the critics say you can't do, and step out into what Jesus has said you can do! And that's everything He did and more!

Remember, they told Jesus He couldn't do them either? Yet He never let that stop Him. It took a cross to stop Him, and that still didn't work!!

We must also remember why the power of the Holy Spirit was, and is still given today to those who believe. It is given for power to be witnesses! Remember we don't "do" witnessing; we are to "be" witnesses. So if the power stopped somewhere, than the witnessing would have had to as well. For the power is given to be witnesses! **"But you will receive power when the Holy Spirit comes on you; and you <u>will be my witnesses</u> in Jerusalem, and in all Judea and Samaria, and <u>to the ends of the earth</u>."** (Acts 1:8)

If this power was only for the early Church than they failed their mission. Why you ask? Well, because they never made it **"to the ends of the earth."** So if Jesus Apostles are gone, and the power with them, then so much for the ends of the Earth right? No, Jesus is very clear in this passage along with Peter later on in Acts 2 that this power is also meant for those who will reach the ends of the Earth! **"This promise is for you and your children and for <u>all</u> who are far off, to as many as the Lord our God will call."** (Acts 2:39) Listen folks, this definitely includes you and I.

In Romans 15:18-19 Paul the Apostle says **"For I will not dare to speak of any of those things which Christ has not accomplished through me, in word and deed, to make the Gentiles obedient in mighty signs and wonders, by the power of the Spirit of God, so that from Jerusalem and round about to Illyricum I have <u>fully preached</u> the gospel of Christ."**

Paul is clearly saying here, that *fully* preaching the Gospel involves a demonstration of mighty signs and wonders, by the power of the Spirit. And so my question is this: If there are no signs and wonders by the power of the Spirit, are we "fully" preaching and demonstrating the Gospel?

I think it's a question people are afraid to ask themselves, but need to. In 1 Corinthians 2:4-5 Paul says, **"My message and my preaching were not with wise and persuasive words, but with a demonstration of the Spirit's power, so that your faith might not rest on men's wisdom, but on God's power."** I'm concerned that much of our faith in today's Church rests upon men's wisdom, more than the power of God. And if anyone understood wise and eloquent teaching, Paul did. It's a well known fact that before He met the Power of God on the road to Damascus, he was well on his way to becoming a Pharisee of Pharisees.

Growing up in the Church, I've continually watched the power of the Word of God, and the power of the Spirit in demonstration, remain in two separate camps. The schools of thought associated with the two, are usually referred to as the Evangelicals, and the Charismatics. The problem is they were never meant to be separate; the early Church was called "the Way" not "the Two Ways" Jesus modeled One Way to live and minister, **"Not by (physical) might, or strength, but by My Spirit, says the Lord."** The early Church operated in both proclamation of the Word, and demonstration of its power by the Spirit.

And when they came across someone not knowing the power, they would teach them. An example of this is found in Acts 18:24-26. **"Meanwhile a Jew named Apollos, a native of Alexandria, came to Ephesus. He was a learned man, with <u>a thorough knowledge of the Scriptures.</u> He had been instructed in the way of the Lord, and he spoke with great fervor and taught about Jesus <u>accurately,</u> though <u>he knew only the baptism of John</u>. He began to speak boldly in the synagogue. When Priscilla and Aquila heard him, they invited him to their home and explained to him <u>the way of God more adequately</u>."**

We can see here that Apollos had a "thorough knowledge of the scriptures", and he, "taught about Jesus accurately." However Priscilla and Aquila saw an inadequacy in his presentation, there was no demonstration of the Word of God in signs and wonders through the power of the Spirit. It says that they then, "…explained to him the Way of God more adequately." **"…the kingdom of God is not a matter of talk but of power." (1 Corinthians 4:20)** So Apollos' message was ACCURATE but apparently not ADEQUATE. Adequate means: sufficient means for a specific requirement or task. Remember what Jesus said in Acts, **"You will receive power to BE my witnesses."** The Greek root of the word "power" here is "dunamis".

It is the word that we derive our modern day word "dynamite" from! It means "with explosive, energy, power or violent force." In Latin it means "potentia" Where we derive our English word "potential".

However, in order for us to walk once again like the Early Church did **"in the same manner as Jesus",** there are two things that need to change. One, is the Charismatic movement needs to rid itself of its pride in coming to know the power, thinking it makes them "better than". They also need to realize, that the purpose for it, is about more than just the gift to speak in other tongues. And two, the Evangelical movement has to get over their fear of the ministry of the Spirit in Power. They need to look into what the scripture clearly teaches regarding Pentecost. And not look only at the foolish extremes that certain groups have made it out to be. It's not about whose better, because no one is.

It's all about the Gospel, and the most effective Way to proclaim and demonstrate it!

I mainly grew up in cessational/evangelical type Churches. And it always bugged me how Pentecost was not really ever talked about, or taught. In fact I don't even remember preachers asking us to turn to the Book of Acts. Yet it was clearly Biblically recorded to be for the Church. I've been in both groups over the years, and all I can see is a separation initiated by man, that was never instituted by God! I've been labeled both, but I call myself a follower of the Way. And the Way is Jesus! And Pentecost is not just for the Pentecostals, it is for ALL WHO BELIEVE!

Priscilla and Aquila never came to Apollos with a "better than" attitude. They simply explained to him a more adequate way to give authority to his preaching by demonstrating it in Power!

Remember the woman with the issue of blood in Mark 5:30? When the woman touched Jesus believing that she would be healed it says, **"At once Jesus felt that power had gone out of him. He turned around in the crowd and asked, "Who touched my clothes?"** So in other words, Jesus was walking through a crowd as he frequently did, but this time, someone needed an explosion in their life, and used the dynamite! Someone accessed the "potentia"! And she accessed it by faith in Jesus! The same way Peter walked on water! The word of God fully preached must involve signs and wonders in the power of the Spirit!

How do you witness in and to a world that fails to acknowledge the Bible as the authoritive Word of God? They don't care about what we have to "say" if we're not backing it up with what we "do"! I like debates in general, but the problem is debates never really produce disciples. Debates almost always lead to confusion, anger, and what the scriptures refer to as **"fruitless discussion"** that will **"shipwreck its hearers."** True authority is not simply announced, it is demonstrated. Authority is always demonstrative. The reason Jesus was known for being, **"one who speaks with authority"** was because following His teaching, He would do what He taught!

In Mark 2:10-12 Jesus said, **"But that you may know that the Son of Man has authority on earth to forgive sins . . . ."** **He said to the paralytic, "I tell you, get up, take your mat and go home." He got up, took his mat and walked out in full view of them all. This amazed everyone and they praised God, saying, "We have never seen anything like this!"** They had never seen anything like what? A paralytic get up and walk? Yes, but also, seeing someone who practiced what they preached!

Folks, what gives authority to the Word of God for someone who doubts its authority? Having a debate perhaps? No! A demonstration of its power!

When a stick of dynamite goes off, you get people's attention!

People gather around to SEE what in the world is going on! People of God, this is the adequate way to preach the Gospel! It's the Way Jesus preached the Gospel! Not too unlike Apollos, in today's Church we "know the scriptures thoroughly" and we fervently "teach about Jesus accurately" but we're doing it inadequately.

It's like we're stuck at John's water baptism for repentance from "dead works", and not receiving and walking in the baptism of the Spirit of power to do life works! Jesus came to give us life more abundantly! 2 Peter 1:3 says that, **"His divine power has given us everything we need for life and godliness through our knowledge of him (Jesus) who called us by his own glory and goodness."** Godliness is a shortened form of God-likeness meaning: to become more like God.

God always demonstrates what He says He will do, therefore He's made us through Jesus to become more like Him, to do what we say! James tells us that he will show us his faith by what he does. And that faith **"without works"** or "demonstration" is not really faith! Peter believed Jesus when he said, "Come "and got "out of the boat", he didn't stay in the boat thinking about the fact that Jesus said he could come. This is one of my major issues with the nature of our present theological mindset.

We see hundreds of students go through seminaries year after year training them to know (head knowledge) what Jesus said in scripture. For instance, you can "Come" to me on the water. The problem is that, few if any, ever demonstrate getting out of the boat. And we then train others to do the same! It's like we all sit in the boat thinking about what it would be like to step out onto the water like Jesus is already doing, but we never do it! This is what bothered me about the whole WWJD fad that went around the Church some years back. It was once again successful in getting us to think about What Jesus Would Do, yet few actually even tried doing what He did! It should have been DWJD, Do What Jesus Did!

It's only when we know in our hearts that we will get out of the boat. The heart is every person's place of belief, intent and motive. It is the place within us in which we do things out of. This is why Jesus said, "It's not what goes into a man that makes him unclean, but that which comes out of him." If the word is known in your heart; then there will be transformation and you will eventually act on it outwardly! If you're not acting on it, then it simply remains information in your head. Remember, the world isn't looking for more information; we have plenty of that. What they're looking for is transformation! We therefore study the Word of God to be transformed, not just to be informed.

This is why Paul and Jesus both said, **"If you believe in your heart."** When we believe in our hearts, it's as good as done, because whatever we do outwardly begins in our hearts. This is why Jesus warns us men not to look at a woman in a manner so as to lust for her IN OUR HEART.

Our hearts are the place of motive and intent!

However, it's like the Church has to *tell* the world that we're different. When you truly are different, you won't have to tell people you are, because they will see it! You shouldn't have to tell people you have authority, they should see it! Jesus didn't just tell people He had authority, he demonstrated it! If you tell people you have something yet never prove it, they'll laugh at you. And unfortunately that's what the world is doing in view of the present day Church; they're laughing! Let's just own it. Let's just get real, and quit kidding ourselves!

However, it wasn't always this way. We see recorded in Acts 5:12-14 that, **"The apostles performed many miraculous signs and wonders among the people. And all the believers used to meet together in Solomon's Colonnade. Many feared joining them, even though they were highly regarded by the people. Even so, more and more men and women believed in the Lord and were added to their number."**

This record of our birth as the Church of Jesus Christ stands in great contrast to the way we look as the Church today. Why are we not seeing this? Why does it seem like no one notices, or is it maybe no one cares to notice? Have you ever noticed that the questions no one wants to ask, usually involve answers every one of us long to have? If we would just admit it, many of us are tired of a weak and emasculated representation of the Church. The Church was never meant to be a weak, if not, dead institution in the world.

It was meant to be a force to be reckoned with! A community of power meant to be noticed, with a message that **"turns the world upside down" (Acts 17:6)** and puts **"the city into an uproar" (Acts 16:20)** and turns a gathering into **"a riot"! (Acts 17:5)** Wherever Jesus went, He never went unnoticed. Why? Because wherever He went, dynamite exploded (dunamis power). Wherever the Early Church went, dynamite exploded!

Exploding dynamite never goes unnoticed!

Yet how much does the Church of today simply go unnoticed? And if we are noticed, it is not usually in a way we should be noticed. For example; one more Church leader gets added to the roster of those caught in immorality or greed. And then it's all over the news. In this case I don't think the old adage "Any press is, good press" works out in our favor.

THE TWO INHIBITING QUESTIONS

So we should now know, that by His power, is how God wants us to live. So what's stopping us? One question I get all the time from people when teaching on this is, "Well what if nothing happens?" I always respond with this, "That's not the right question." The right question is, "What if something does happen?"

I remember listening to a preacher one time who had prayed for 19 people who were blind, and none of their eyes were opened. He said, "I could have stopped at 19 and came to the conclusion from my own experience that, 'It's just not God's will'. Then he said, "But my conclusion would have been inconclusive with what the Word of God says. So my conclusion would be wrong." Guess what happened? The 20th blind person he prayed for, had their eyes opened! He said, "I was just as surprised as they were!"

You see the Word of God determines God's will, not our experiences or lack of. The principle here is this. We MUST base what we believe and do on what God has said in His word, not from what we do, or do not experience. That's why it's called faith. God said it, and we have faith in that He will do what He said! If our experience lines up with the Word and character of God as revealed in scripture then great! If it doesn't then we question the experience, not the Word of God. Our society allows its "world view" to form what it calls truth. The problem with this is that, the truth should be forming our world view, not the other way around.

Now the other question that inhibits us from action is, "Well what will people think?" My answer to this is, "Who cares!" If Jesus was so concerned about what other people thought, He would never have done the things He did! Don't forget that King Saul lost his position as King, and his kingdom, due to the fear of what the people thought. The fear of man debilitated him in obeying the commands of God! Proverbs 29:25 says, **"The Fear of man will prove to be a snare, but whoever trusts in the Lord is kept safe."**

If Jesus was to be able to obey the Father, which He did, he had to refuse giving in to the fear of man. The same goes for us. If we are going to obey the Word of God, and the inner leading of His still small voice, we must refuse to entertain the fear of what people might think! And I say "might think" because half the time people aren't even thinking what you think they're thinking anyway! So get over it, and get on with proclaiming and demonstrating!

KEEPING THE TANK FULL

Jesus, full of the Holy Spirit, returned from the Jordan, And was led in the Spirit in the wilderness. (Luke 4:1)

And the disciples were continually being filled with joy and with the Holy Spirit. (Acts 13:52)

One principle of following Jesus in "the Way" that cannot be overlooked, is that of being continually filled with the Spirit. The filling and coming upon of the "power from on high" is NOT a onetime occurrence! The scriptures are clear that we need to continually be filled with the Spirit!

Whenever you give out a resource you need to get more if you plan on continuing to give out that resource. It's called "supply and demand". It's a principle that we operate by every day in the world, and the same principle applies in the Kingdom of God. When a rechargeable battery cell expends its energy, it needs to be recharged! There's no usable energy unless there's a recharge. I believe this is why we see Jesus in the scriptures, **"...often going off alone to be with the Father"**. Remember, He walked as we ourselves now do, as an ordinary man filled with the Holy Spirit and Power!

I have noticed in many Pentecost circles that the thought maintained is that you're only "clothed with power from on high "in a onetime event. But the scriptural fact of the matter is if we're continually pouring out, we need a continual pouring in! Of course that's another issue in itself, are we pouring out? Remember, Jesus said that the Baptism of Power was for us to become witnesses. Witnesses share what they have. Far too often it's downgraded to a personal experience of the Holy Ghost goose bumps. This was never, and will never, be its purpose.

Yes, we are meant to experience it personally, but it was never meant to remain exclusively a personal experience. It was and is given to equip you with more than adequate means in proclaiming and demonstrating the Gospel, the Power of God unto salvation for the world!

Pentecost was never meant to become a single denomination; but an experience to equip all believers!

A SEPARATE EXPERIENCE

Many evangelical theologians take the position that there is only one baptism offered in the life of a believer, John's. John's baptism, as most of us know, was one of water. Which speaks of cleansing. It's a public declaration of our dying to sin, and resurrection with Christ. My problem with this viewpoint of it being "the only baptism" is that even John the Baptist spoke of another baptism that was now available through Jesus' ministry.

John said, **"I indeed baptize you with water unto repentance, but He who is coming after me is mightier than I, whose sandals I am not worthy to carry. And He will baptize you with the Holy Spirit and fire. (Matthew 3:11)** I'm sorry, but we'd have to be blind to not see that John himself just referred to more than one baptism! With water, Holy Spirit, and Fire. If anything, there are three: water, Spirit, and Fire. Fire of course, is mainly used in scripture to mean purification.

What appeared on the believers in the upper room on the Day of Pentecost when they received the Baptism of the Spirit? Fire! Despite the belief that the baptism of the Spirit is received when you get saved, it is plainly referred to in scripture as two separate instances. Even though they can happen simultaneously, it doesn't seem to be altogether common. (Example: Cornelius' Household) In John 20: 17-21 we see that Jesus appeared to the disciples after He went before the Father. Why would He have to go to the Father first? It's simple, salvation is God's.

The Power Vested in Us

Jesus purchased our salvation through the cross. In doing things in order, as is God's way, Jesus had to go to the Father to get the salvation that He purchased from the Father by His own blood sacrifice. In Psalm 20:66 David says, **"Now I know that the Lord saves his anointed; he answers him from his holy heaven with <u>the saving power</u> of <u>his right hand</u>."**

This is why the scripture tells us that Jesus now sits at the right hand of God, He obtained salvation, and salvation belongs in Gods eyes, at His right hand. After this, John then tells us that Jesus **"breathed on them and they received the Holy Spirit."** He in that moment spoke nothing of power "dunamis", He only spoke of forgiveness from sin. Why? It's because this was the receiving the Holy Spirit as "the seal of salvation", not the clothing of "power from on high". He spoke of forgiving other's as they had themselves just received forgiveness.

Now, if they were one in the same event, Jesus would not have told them to go and wait in the upper room for something else later. The disciples at this point were born again. Jesus gave them the salvation that He obtained from the Father. Notice Jesus breathed on them. Breath in this instance was "new spirit" and "new life".

Then we hear Jesus in Acts 1:3-5 giving a "command" not a "suggestion". **"On one occasion, while he was eating with them, he gave them this <u>command</u>: "Do not leave Jerusalem, but wait for the gift my Father promised, which you have heard me speak about. For John baptized with water, but in a few days you will be baptized with the Holy Spirit."** Once again we see two baptisms referred to here, not one. If the disciples already received "the power from on high" when He breathed on them, why would He have them expecting a second event? That line of logic is not logical, nor is it scriptural for that matter.

COMPLETELY FULL COMPLETELYADEQUATE

Now the disciples were completely adequate to administer the Kingdom in the same manner as Jesus Himself did, <u>full</u> of the Holy Spirit and Power! We see this in Acts 4:13-14 **"Now when they (the Pharisees) saw the boldness of Peter and John, and had perceived that they were <u>unlearned</u> and <u>ignorant</u> men, they marveled; and they took note that <u>they had been with Jesus</u>. And seeing the man that was healed standing with them, <u>they could say nothing against it</u>."**

I love this, when there's a demonstration of the Power of God, there's nothing man can say against it! There's a lot to be said in a debate, but a demonstration of the Kingdom of God silences the scoffers and skeptics. And to top it off, all this power was operating in and through "unlearned and ignorant men"! Thank God He uses "the weak to confound the wise" that means we all have a chance, and no one has to be left out! Hallelujah! You don't have to get a $100,000 student loan and spend 4 years in a classroom getting your Masters in Theology first. You only have to believe, freely receive, and freely give! As you study the scriptures, the Holy Spirit through the Word and in your own spirit will teach you all you need to know. (1 John 27)

IT'S YOUR RESPONSIBILITY

"If you then, though you are not good, know how to give good gifts to your children, how much more will your Father in heaven give the Holy Spirit to those who <u>ASK</u> him?" (Luke 11:13)

Okay, just so we're clear, it's your responsibility to ask Holy Spirit to fill you up each and every day. It is NOT your Pastors, or any Ministry Leader's responsibility, it is yours. And you cannot wait for the next conference to come along.

You need Him now! Ask Him to fill you each and every day, to do what He has called you to do that day!

GET YOUR OWN BREAD

We seem to have what I call "Conference Junkies" in the Church. They have to get to the next big conference, to hear the next big anointed minister, and get them to lay hands on them, to impart something that supposedly takes them to the next level in their spirituality. Folks this is not how it works!

Listen I believe in impartation as much as the next person, but a believer cannot live on someone else's bread all the time. There comes a time when you have to get your own bread. Constantly seeking impartation is dangerous. And quite frankly it's exposes laziness in the body of Christ towards seeking God for themselves. I'll never forget when I heard Pastor George Hill of Victory Churches International share this story. He said, "I had a gentleman come up to me at an altar call one time and said, 'Pastor George, I believe you have a word for me.'" Pastor George promptly replied, "Yes I do, read your Bible."

You see, the Lord revealed to Pastor Hill in an instant that this man was going around seeking words from men, yet not seeking God's own word. In the same manner as Jesus with the woman at the well, the Holy Spirit revealed to Pastor Hill something about this man that he never knew through natural wisdom. It was what the Bible calls a word of knowledge The gentlemen wanted to eat everyone else's bread, and wasn't willing to get his own.

This reminds me of the old Tale of the Little Red Hen: *One day as the Little Red Hen was scratching in a field, she found a grain of wheat."This wheat should be planted," she said. "Who will plant this grain of wheat?" "Not I," said* the Duck. "Not I," said the Cat. "Not I," said the Dog. "Then I will," said the Little Red Hen. And she did. Soon the wheat grew to be tall and yellow. "

The wheat is ripe," said the Little Red Hen. "Who will cut the wheat?" "Not I," said the Duck. "Not I," said the Cat. "Not I," said the Dog. "Then I will," said the Little Red Hen. And she did. When the wheat was cut, the Little Red Hen said, "Who will thresh the wheat?" "Not I," said the Duck. "Not I," said the Cat. "Not I," said the Dog. "Then I will," said the Little Red Hen.

And she did. When the wheat was threshed, the Little Red Hen said, "Who will take this wheat to the mill?" "Not I," said the Duck. "Not I," said the Cat. "Not I," said the Dog. "Then I will," said the Little Red Hen. And she did. She took the wheat to the mill and had it ground into flour. Then she said, "Who will make this flour into bread?" "Not I," said the Duck. "Not I," said the Cat. "Not I," said the Dog." Then I will," said the Little Red Hen. And she did. She made and baked the bread.

Then she said, "Who will eat this bread?""Oh! I will," said the Duck. "And I will," said the Cat."And I will," said the Dog."No, No!" said the Little Red Hen. "I will do that." And she did. (The Gingerbread Guide: Using Folktales with Young Children. Copyright 1987 Scott, Foresman and Company.)

The whole point of this tale of course, is that no one wants to do the prep work, but they all want to eat the finished bread. Folks, we need to watch out for this attitude in the Church. I've talked to many ministry leader's who are very frustrated with this mentality, and I don't blame them, it's not right! People will spend a lot of time and thousands of dollars on flights, hotels and registration fees to get to the newest Church conference that's offering fresh bread. The problem is; they don't realize the amount of work it took that Church to make the bread. It most likely took years of tears, prayer, fasting, evangelism, and faithfulness in serving to name a few. But "Conference Junkies" don't want much to do with that stuff; they just want the finished product, the bread. They want a quick impartation of what it took that Church years of prayer and faithfulness to obtain. People of God, we need to stop finding someone else to feed us, and start doing the work to feed ourselves!

A baby needs someone to feed them, an adult works to feed them self. Get the picture? In Hebrews 6:1 it says, **"Anyone who lives on milk, is a baby..."** Those who feed on milk, need it fed to them, but those eating solid food, are able to feed themselves. If you've been a believer for 2 or more years now, you need to start feeding yourself. I'm so tired of hearing the same excuse, "Well, we left that Church because we weren't getting fed." Listen, all the Shepherd (Pastor) does is lead the sheep to the pasture, he doesn't shove the grass down their throats. So grow up and feed yourself!

No, they feed on the grass on their own. The only ones the Shepherd feeds Himself are the newborn lambs. And that's because they aren't mature enough yet to feed on grass by themselves, they need to be fed milk. We all need to know what the Word of God says personally, you can't live off of what you hear from other people alone; this includes your Pastor. How are we to know which thoughts, ideas, and philosophies are false, and need to be cast down, if we don't know the Word of God enough for ourselves to refute them? Your Pastor won't always be available for tech support! And by the way, they didn't become a Pastor to do the studying and learning, so you wouldn't have to. They did it to equip you to do it for yourself!

It amazes me the number of people that think that just because the Pastor is in the "paid position", it's their responsibility to do it all! No wonder so many leaders burn out!

Jesus told us to pray, **"Give us this day <u>our</u> daily bread."** Did you notice He didn't say "Give us this day someone else's daily bread"? So it's clear, we are to ask for a daily word from the Word of God, and ask for the filling of the Spirit daily to maintain a full tank. Many times in scripture we see that those disciples who did amazing exploits were by no coincidence "full of the Spirit" when they did them.

Even when they needed someone to wait tables in Acts 6:3, which we might consider to be a menial task, Paul said, **"…choose seven men from among you who are known to be <u>full of the Spirit</u> and wisdom."** Remember, like a battery, you cannot expend energy unless you are full of energy. The followers of Jesus stayed charged up through study, prayer and request.

And it's no different for us today, we stay full of the Spirit through study, prayer and request. A good example of this is found in Acts 4:29-31. We see that persecution from the Chief Priests and elders due to the Gospel was becoming a long hard road for the disciples. And their tanks were reaching the empty mark. So they turned to the Lord in prayer and request.

"Now, Lord, consider their threats and enable your servants to speak your word with great boldness. Stretch out your hand to heal and perform miraculous signs and wonders through the name of your holy servant Jesus." After they prayed, the place where they were meeting was shaken. And <u>they were all filled</u> with the Holy Spirit and spoke the word of God boldly."

Notice they were *ALL* filled with the Spirit? Not just Peter and John "the Apostles". So we can see that the Disciples practiced proclamation, demonstration, and filling station! Again folks, we are called to walk in the same way. The very word "disciple" means "disciplined one or one who follows a certain discipline." Whoever's discipline a disciple follows, that person becomes their Master in that discipline.

Jesus disciples followed His discipline, so He was their Master. So the question now is, "What disciplines did Jesus model for us?" He modeled fervent prayer, fasting, demonstrative proclamation of the Gospel of the Kingdom of God, and right living by the Spirit to name a few. So when we hear Jesus tell us things to do in scripture, if we truly are His disciples and followers, then we need to follow in His disciplines. If He is indeed our Master, then we should do what He says, right? Well then, why do so many folks read what Jesus has told them to do, and then contextualize their way out of doing it?

It's like if people don't feel comfortable with what Jesus said to do, they say, "Well what Jesus really meant was this..." and they'll proceed to interpret His commands to an end they will be comfortable with. It worries me when people feel they can take the parts of the Bible they like, and disregard the parts they don't like. It's nothing new however, it's actually a journalist technique called "selective omission". It's when you purposely leave out information from an event because it doesn't support your viewpoint. I don't know about you, but to me, this sounds a lot like living a lie.

According to scripture, I feel it's clear that Jesus has commanded us to be baptized in water, as well as **"...wait for the promise of the Father"** to be baptized in the Holy Spirit and Power! And for us to remember, that it's our responsibility alone to keep the tank full on a regular basis.

If I don't sense assistance from the Holy Spirit whatsoever in my Christian walk, it's not God's fault, or anyone else's if I haven't asked for the power. Remember, the only one who can hold you back from seeking God, and keeping your tank full; is you.

In order for us to fulfill the mandate of the Kingdom of God on Earth, we MUST be full of the Spirit and Power! Remember Zechariah 4:6? It's how the Kingdom functions and how God does everything He does. "Not by (physical) might nor by power, but by my Spirit,' says the Lord Almighty." Also remember what it says in Romans 8:11, **"And if the Spirit of him who raised Jesus from the dead is living in you, he who raised Christ from the dead will also give life to your mortal bodies through his Spirit, who lives in you."** Folks this does not only mean life for resurrection later, but it also means life to your body now! God wants you to be full of His life every day! Not just for you, for others you come in contact with every day!

CHAPTER 4

Operating and Maintaining the Vehicle

Physical training does have value, but godliness has value for all things, holding promise for both the present life, and the life to come.

1 Timothy 4:7-8

Do you not know that your body is a temple of the Holy Spirit, who is in you, whom you have received from God? You are not your own; you were bought at a price. Therefore honor God with your body.

1 Corinthians 6:19-20

THE OUTER MAN

I had not planned on a Chapter about this, but the Lord really impressed it upon my heart while writing this book, to deal with the topic. And that is this. If your body was indeed purposed to be a vehicle for the presence of God, then just like any vehicle, we need to maintain it so it doesn't break down. A broken down car isn't going anywhere, therefore it cannot fulfill its purpose.

When we live in such an incredibly driven society as we do today, it's hard not to get stressed out, physically worn down, or to develop sickness and or disease. Medical society has recently discovered and determined that the cause of many sicknesses and diseases can be attributed to stress, worry, lack of physical rest and exercise.

I heard one Christian physician say, that he believes many problems Christians struggle with today, have more to do with physical issues, than spiritual ones. The average person works far more than the recommended weekly hours. Few, if any, take a full day to physically rest. And many eat a daily diet based on their currently driven lifestyle. All of these are completely unhealthy! I don't know about you, but I have noticed a major increase lately in the number of cases of cancer.

It seems like hardly a day goes by that we do not hear about someone else who found out that they have cancer. Still, it's like no one notices, or doesn't want to notice that it wasn't always like this. I asked an older gentleman one time if cancer was as widespread back in his day as it is today. Of course he said, "No, not at all." So if it wasn't always like this, then that means that something has changed somewhere along the way. One thing my wife and I noticed, was the odd ingredients found in many of the prepared foods we buy at the grocery store. It's like you have to understand another language to even pronounce them. And when you do an internet search, you find out what I find to be very disturbing, it's not even a food, it's a chemical! Hello! A chemical!

I was eating a bowl of my favorite cereal while working on my laptop one evening, and a popup displayed on a website that asked me, "Do You Know What You're Eating?" I believe God will use any available means to speak to us at any time, and He did! So I decided to read the ingredients on the cereal box. The only ones I recognized or could even read for that matter were corn and sugar. And this was out of the 20 or so ingredients listed! So needless to say, I threw out the cereal.

And to be completely honest, I was very disturbed by the fact that my government approved such a product for my consumption that was easily over 50% chemicals! I mean think about that for minute. And this I think leads us to one of the culprits in the position that "something has changed".

And we know that this is the case with much of the food products available on the market today. I firmly believe that the old saying "You are what you eat" really holds true in this case for sure. So we are eating chemicals that we are now coming to know cause cancer, and then when people get cancer, we try to beat it with guess what? Chemicals! You would never fill your vehicles tank with vinegar. No, of course not, it would destroy the engine. The engine was designed to consume gas, not vinegar. Likewise, the human body was never meant to consume chemicals!

JESUS WALKED IN DIVINE HEALTH

The point of this, is that we are responsible for what we put into our bodies. After all, we are the temple of God! The "body" of Christ! So this brings me to my next point. Remember how the Israelites were always blessed when the Ark was present? Well don't you think that you would be blessed as well with His Presence actually living in you? Of course! Let me ask you a question.

How many sick days did Jesus take? The immediate and undeniable answer to that is none.

So if I'm to walk in the same manner as Jesus did, as commanded by John, then sick days shouldn't be an issue for me either. You say, "Yeah, but that was Jesus!" Let me remind you again, Peter being an ordinary man did what Jesus was doing and walked on the water too. And he only became unable to do so when he doubted by looking instead at his unstable surroundings.

The Bible says that, *"... we have become partakers of His divine nature."* And that, **"He has given us everything we need for life and godliness."** **(2 Peter 1:3-4)** I believe that Gods divine nature in us gives us the ability to walk in divine health just like Jesus did! But like everything else in the Christian life, it is only realized and experienced by faith!

I believe this so much so that I pray this over my family and our Church every night, *"That we would walk in the divine health, life, and nature of Jesus Himself, who not one day fell to sickness or disease. He who Himself walked in the weakness of flesh and blood as we do. So I declare over us that no sickness, disease, virus or allergy has any right to ever enter or operate in our bodies! Bless us with long life on Earth Lord, that we die old, full of days, wealth and wisdom. In Jesus mighty name... Amen!"*

I know... I know... the first thing that's pops into the unrenewed mind is, "You can't say that you'll never be sick, there are viruses and stuff going around all the time!" That's true, but it doesn't mean you have to just accept them now does it? Just as much as Jesus was tempted in all ways common to man, yet didn't sin. His body was bombarded every day with germs and viruses like we are, He even touched lepers! Yet He was never sick. How can this be? Because He chose not to accept either one...ever! We can choose too!

Ever since my family and I came to realize this truth, and stand in faith for it, we've gone through three flu seasons unaffected! I believe that just as Peter chose to walk atop the water by faith in Jesus, we can walk above sin, sickness and disease by faith in Jesus. However, unlike Peter who fell to the fear of his surroundings, **"Let us fix our eyes on Jesus, the author and perfecter of our faith..."** **(Hebrews 12:2)**

Let us be those who declare with David, **"A thousand may fall at my side, ten thousand at my right hand, but it will not come near me."** (Psalm 91:7) And also agree with Jesus that, **"Everything is possible for him who believes!"** (Mark 9:23) Even though we may be surrounded by sickness and disease as Peter was surrounded by the storm, we don't have to fall into the fear of getting them.

There's a well known account of a preacher named John G. Lake operating in this while ministering in South Africa. While assisting doctors during a bubonic plague outbreak, he was asked why he had not contracted the disease since he had used none of their medical protection. He answered with this, "It is the Spirit of life in Christ Jesus." To demonstrate, he had them take live bubonic plague germs still foaming from the lungs of a newly dead person and put them on his hand and then examine the germs under a microscope. They were dying on his skin!

However you have to keep up your end of things. You can't expect divine health and healing if you're living a lifestyle that's destructive to your health! You have to keep things in balance. Sleep and eat right, live healthy, study, pray, request and minister. Jesus lived like this, and so can we! **"Therefore honor God with your body."** (1 Corinthians 6:20) A sick body never brings glory to God! So why do so many in the Church believe this! I would never teach my child a lesson by injecting him with a sickness or disease! So how much more would a loving God never do such a thing! (Read Matthew 7:9-11)

Watching someone else suffer in agony would NEVER cause me to seek to know their god! And it certainly wouldn't cause me to give honor to that god. This is once again a scripturally ridiculous idea! The bible fully supports us suffering against fleshly temptations, and trials and persecution from others for the sake of the Gospel, but never from sickness and disease!

You don't have to get sick to minister to someone in a hospital, just go minister in a hospital! And if God wants you there, He can get you in without making you sick. We must never forget Jesus never died of sickness; he died because He alone chose to lay down His life for our sin! And in His death, He dealt with sin and sickness once and for all so we wouldn't have to. So believe it, receive it, and walk in the finished work of the cross! Jesus came to save and heal; they are both a part of the atonement!

READ YOUR SERVICE MANUAL

"Remember the word to Your servant, upon which You have caused me to hope. This is my comfort in my troubles, for Your word gives me life." (Psalms 119:49-50) Believe it or not, your Bible is the manual for your vehicle, the body. Some nutritionists have even begun to realize that many of the foods and grains that have been found to be the most beneficial to the human body have also been laid out in scripture as healthy. In Ezekiel 4:9 the Lord prescribes this combination of grains in one bread for the prophet to eat, **"Also take for yourself wheat, barley, beans, lentils, millet, and spelt; put them into one vessel, and make bread of them for yourself."**

After all, God made our bodies, so I'm quite sure He knows what foods cause them to operate the best! David said, **"Your word gives me life."** God's word can't help but bring life! For God Himself is life! When He speaks, He speaks life! His word always produces its purpose. That's why if we are to be like Him, we need to speak life, to bless and not curse. **"...the tongue of the wise brings healing." Proverbs 12:18**

When you read and meditate on the word of God, you cannot help but be invigorated spiritually, and physically!

Psalms 107:20 says, **"He sent forth his word and healed them; and he rescued them from the grave."** If we appropriate it, God's Word can heal us and guard us from premature death. And like the forefathers of the faith we too can die "old and full of days."

Pastor Hazel Hill of Victory Churches International has written a book of prayers called "Praying God's Word". I highly recommend this book! She wrote it out of experiencing the word of God healing her and saving her from an early grave. On the tape series derived from the book she says, *"Many people will spend hundreds of dollars on pharmaceuticals, and faithfully take them three times a day, but few will take the word of God which is free, and prescribe it even once a day towards their healing."* Folks we need to follow the manual! The manufacturer always knows their product the best!

He formed every part of you in your mother's womb, so surely He can heal, revive and restore every part that breaks down. Even though you may have a bad report from a doctor, God's report is always greater! Doctor's however, do the best that they can, with the limited resources they have. And absolutely I respect that, and am thankful for them. We have a doctor in our Church for that matter. But even she will agree that no doctor will ever claim to be able to heal you. And that is because they cannot heal you. They can only help promote the natural healing process. But when nothing is successful, and they run out of procedures, the only thing they have left is a terminal diagnosis.

God however declares in Exodus 15:26, **"I am the Lord, who heals you."** And Jesus declared, **"I am the resurrection and the life!" (John 11:25)** No one else can save you, heal you, and resurrect you! The power to perform all of these lies exclusively in the hands of an almighty loving God! He has prescribed to us His word. A manual for an abundant Christian life! However, we must read and know the instructions in order for them to be of any benefit to us.

And by the way, God's corporation has the best benefit plan of all: **"Praise the Lord, O my soul, and do not forget all his benefits. Yes God who forgives <u>all</u> your sins and heals <u>all</u> your diseases." (Psalms 103:2-3)** We must not forget His benefits. So study the company manual people!

Remember it's not your Pastor's responsibility, it's yours! Don't rely on what you've heard from others regarding the manual, read it for yourself! 2 Timothy 2:15 says, **"Study to show yourself approved by God, as a workman that needs not be ashamed, but rightly divides the word of truth."** I cannot stress enough the importance of knowing the word of God!

Even in the natural, you cannot experience any of the benefits of an inheritance if you weren't present for the reading of the will. You have to know the Last Will and Testament in order to experience the inheritance. Why do you think that two of the greatest struggles of any Christian are to read the Bible and pray? Our present enemy, the devil, wants to keep us from knowing our Father's will. For one, he knows that "the Will" contains incriminating evidence against him. And secondly he knows that "the Will" contains all we need to know for "life and godliness." And the last thing he wants is for us to have life, and to become more like the One he hates; God. We already bear too much resemblance as it is!

In Satan's eyes, it's bad enough that we are made in God's image, let alone actually start to act like God too!

You see the devil knows about the Word of God. Remember when he tempted Jesus in the desert? What did he use? He used promises from the scriptures, although he twisted and tweaked them ever so slightly to his agenda; which is to lie. That's always his agenda.

However, Jesus knowing "the truth" resisted the devil out of his submission to God and the truth of His Word. And guess what, the devil fled! Does this sound familiar at all? James 4:7 says, **"Submit yourselves to God. Resist the devil, and he will flee from you."** Once again, we see Jesus setting the example for us in how we should walk "in the manner" that He himself did! He went before us as an example of one resisting the devil from the position of one who obeys God. Listen, you can't resist a flea if you're not submitted to God. Humility and obedience are the two power players in the Kingdom of God!

Remember, Satan lost his glorious position in Heaven because of pride. **"God resist's the proud, but gives grace to the humble."** (James 4:6) And by the way true humility is not thinking less of yourself, it's thinking of yourself less. It's to remain consciously aware of our own weakness and frailty apart from God. It's to have a divine dependence on God for everything, everyday. We cannot live this way without having God intervene in all our daily affairs. In Isaiah 66:2 God says, **"This is the one I esteem: he who is humble and contrite (quick to repent) in spirit, and trembles at my word."** I believe humility itself even plays a role in us walking in divine health. Humility guards us from things like greed and envy. And this is because humility goes hand in hand with thankfulness.

Humble people, tend to be thankful people. Humble people seem to have a peace about them and as Solomon shares with us in Proverbs 14:30, **"A heart at peace gives life to the body..."** And then he says, **"... but envy rots the bones."** We cannot take the first portion of this proverb as literal, and think the second part to be just a saying.

Here's a thought. Osteoporosis is a progressive disease in which the bones gradually become weaker and weaker, causing changes in posture, and causing susceptibility to fractures. I would be interested in seeing a study on patients diagnosed with this condition, and see if we couldn't see a connection between it, and a person who lived their life in jealousy and envy of other's. I would not be surprised at all if we would find a direct connection. This is not to say however, that every one of the case studies would have that connection, but I bet the percentages would be high.

USING THE POWER

Jesus said, "Someone touched me; I know that power has gone out from me." (Luke 8:46)

"My message and my preaching were not with wise and persuasive words, but with a demonstration of the Spirit's power..." (1 Corinthians 2:4)

In the above verse 1 Corinthians 2:4, Paul says it was **"the Spirit's power"**. However, Paul was the one who did the demonstration. We need to realize that the power has nothing to do with us. It's not of our own power, meaning of our own fleshly strength, which is not really strength at all, but weakness for that matter. Nor does it have anything to do with our religious piety. It is purely, and simply, from God. However, the demonstration of that power has everything to do with us.

God Himself has ordained **"the weak to confound the wise"**. This is how He shows His glory. He turns impossibilities into possibilities! But the point I want us to get here is this:

The power is God's; but the responsibility of demonstrating it, has been given to us!

Sorry for this next illustration, but you'll get the point. It's like being a vacuum salesman; you have nothing to do with the creation of the vacuum itself, you simply demonstrate its power, so that those who see it in action will believe it, and buy it! Here are some passages from Acts Chapter 3 giving us a clear picture of this principle. Acts 3:6-8 says, **"Then Peter said, "Silver or gold I do not have, but <u>what I have</u> <u>I give you</u>. In the name of Jesus Christ of Nazareth, walk." Taking him by the right hand, he helped him up, and instantly the man's feet and ankles became strong. He jumped to his feet and began to walk. Then he went with them into the temple courts, walking and jumping, and praising God!"**

Then in verses 11-12, **"While the beggar held on to Peter and John, all the people were astonished and came running to them in the place called Solomon's Colonnade. When Peter saw this, he said to them: "Men of Israel, why does this surprise you? Why do you stare at us as if by our own power or godliness we had made this man walk?"** Then they were questioned by the religious leaders. They asked them by what power or by what name had they done this. In verse 16 they answered them saying, **"Faith in His name (Jesus), has made this man strong, whom you see and know. Yes, the faith which comes through Him has given him this perfect soundness in the presence of you all."**

You see, Peter and John are very clear that they were not the source of the power; however, the use of that power was clearly demonstrated through them. Peter said in verse 6, **"But what I have, I GIVE YOU!"** Notice they didn't sit and talk to the beggar about the fact that God could heal him, they demonstrated it! Peter and John preached the Gospel in power, the way it was and is really meant to be proclaimed. For too long, the North American Church at least, has presented a wimpy Gospel! We try to give our best presentation of how scary Hell is, and that you don't want to go there, so you better get saved! It's like, there's really no fear of God anymore, so getting people to fear going to Hell was our back up plan. Folks this is not a biblical model for presenting the Gospel at all!

The book of Acts records very clearly, that people were radically saved out of a reverent fear of God, not the fear of Hell!

In Acts 5:11-15 it says, **"So great fear came upon all the church and upon all who heard these things. And through the hands of the apostles many signs and wonders were done among the people. And they were all with one accord in Solomon's Porch. Yet none of the rest dared join them, but the people esteemed them highly. And believers were increasingly added to the Lord, multitudes of both men and women..."** The scripture doesn't say that, "The fear of Hell is the beginning of wisdom." It says that, **"The fear of the Lord is the beginning of wisdom, and knowledge of the Holy One is understanding." (Proverbs 9:10)** Why is it wise to fear God?

It's wise to fear Him because He is the All in All. There is true life and salvation found in no one else but God alone. He holds the universe in His hands, so for what reason would I fear anyone, or anything else. Why fear men, when

God was the one who made them? Why fear the devil, when God has completely stripped Him of all power? And why fear death, when Christ in you has triumphed victoriously over death and the grave!

The Good News is all about God and His power! Not Hell and it's torment.

The gospel is, **"the power of God unto salvation."** We are to preach the message that the kingdom of heaven is near, so turn from sin by turning to God for salvation! Unfortunately we've made the Gospel into a "How You Can Escape Hell" message rather than the "How You Can Gain the Kingdom" message that Jesus himself preached straight out of the desert. **"From that time on Jesus began to preach, "Repent, for the kingdom of heaven is near." (Matthew 4:17)**

Jesus never tried to scare people with Hell-fire and brimstone, but what He said, and did, caused people to stand in awe of God, and fear Him alone! We shouldn't stand in awe of Hell; we should stand in awe of God! However the question remains, *"How can people stand in awe of the Power of God, if it's not being demonstrated?"* God has chosen, and ordained us, His Church to be the conduits of His power on Earth.

As with Moses, through us God wants to, **"show His wonders."** But too many times we either suppress the Holy Spirit's leading, or we more seriously **"deny the power therein."** Folks, this needs to change! Growing up in the Church I've grown tired of our weak and often futile presentations of the Gospel. In fact, I think it begs the question that if it's not presented in power, then is it the Full Gospel? If it is, it certainly doesn't seem to line up with the many clear examples of the presentation of the Gospel as recorded in the Bible.

Listen, do you honestly think that the power God has given you, was just meant for you? I don't think so. That's not the way of the Kingdom! The way of the kingdom is to give. Jesus laid this out for us when He said in Matthew 10:6-8, **"As you go, preach this message: 'The kingdom of heaven is near.' Heal the sick, raise the dead, and cleanse those who have leprosy, drive out demons. Freely you have received, now freely give."** God has freely given you the Kingdom, but it's up to you to give it, or release it! God won't do it for you, and that's because, what you have received is now in your hands, and subject to your will! **"The spirit of the prophet is subject to the prophet."** (1 Corinthians 14:32)

Your own spirit is subject to you. You have control over your own spirit. Just as much as you do over your soul (mind, will and emotions) and your body. This is why we're not seeing the power demonstrated folks! It's not being released! It's like we're all walking around keeping the Kingdom of God hidden within us! What did Jesus say regarding this? I recall Him saying something like this, **"You are the light of the world. A city on a hill cannot be hidden. Neither do people light a lamp and put it under a bowl. Instead they put it on its stand, and it gives light to everyone in the house. In the same way, let your light shine before men, that they may see your good deeds and praise your Father in heaven."** (Matthew 5:14-16) Notice Jesus said "...that they may see your good deeds"? He wasn't just referring to carrying the lady next door's groceries, although that's good too. He was referring to doing the things that He did, and people saw Him doing.

In Acts 10:37-38 Peter says, **"For you all know what has happened throughout Judea, beginning in Galilee, after the baptism that John preached. And of how God anointed Jesus of Nazareth with the Holy Spirit and power, and how he went around doing good and healing all who were** under the power of the devil, because God was with him." Jesus went about "doing good and healing *ALL* who were under the power of the devil". What was He doing? Letting His light shine before all men! We're to do the same. So how did He do it? Well, God anointed Him with the Holy Spirit, and power!

We also have been given the Holy Spirit and power through the Pentecost experience available to all who believe today, and up until Christ returns! Oh, but it also says that God was with Him. Folks what does the word Emmanuel mean? It means: God with us! Hallelujah! Say no more! Listen; if you're a believer and have received the power from on high, then God has anointed you with the Holy Spirit and power to go about doing good, healing all those oppressed under the power of the devil because God is with you! Jesus laid aside all His divine attributes to walk in the weakness of flesh, anointed with the Holy Spirit and power! He did it as an example for us to do the same.

And He also abolished the sin, that is in the flesh, by taking it to the grave Himself in His own body. (**See Hebrews 2:14&15**) Therefore, we have no excuse not to walk and live like Jesus; for we have been given all the tools He himself used. So what it comes down to is this, we either do not know about the tools we've been given, or we do know, yet simply refuse to use them. If you didn't know about the tools up to this point, it's understandable. However, you now know. So what will you do with them? If you have known about the tools and have not wanted to use them; why? Are you afraid of the promised persecution? Are you afraid it won't work? Are you afraid of what your Church might think? Did you notice every question I asked had to do with fear?

There's a reason for that. I believe that fear is the main reason people aren't stepping out into the lifestyle of doing what Jesus did. But here's the dilemma. Whatever the fear is that is holding you back, the scripture is very clear that we are to fear God and Him alone. You see when we fear God; we have no cause to fear anything or anyone else, because the fear of the Lord drives out all other fears! And when we fear God and therefore come to Him, we find out that He is love.

1 John 4:18 says that, **"There is no fear in love. But perfect love drives out fear, because fear has to do with torment. The one who fears is not made perfect in love."** Just like the words of the old renowned hymn Amazing Grace. "It was grace that taught my heart to fear, and grace my fears relieved." Jesus knew he was loved by the Father, so He had no fear. Sons and daughters of God know this: God loves you, you have no need to fear, He doesn't want to torment you, He wants to save you! Allow His love to drive out all other fears to the point that you only stand in awe of God alone. And then walk in the same manner that Christ Himself did!

NOT OF THIS WORLD, BUT STILL IN IT

Have you ever wondered why when you get saved you're not just instantly in Heaven with Jesus? I mean if it's true, the way the majority of the Church seems to view Christianity, that we're just sitting back and waiting to go to heaven when we die. If Heaven is only what it's all about, then why do we have to wait 'til we die to go? Why not, you get saved, and BOOM! you're in Heaven! The answer is because you're still in this World for a reason. And by the way Heaven is coming to us for that matter. Christ is coming to rule and reign for eternity on Earth, and us with Him. This is what scripture teaches, the Kingdom of God, coming to Earth.

However, I don't have the time in this book to get into that at this point. But the Church is now starting to realize it anyways. There has been an incredible increase even recently of teaching on the coming of the Kingdom of God. Why? I believe it's because we're closer than ever before to the Return of the King! No, not Lord of the Rings, the Lord of All, Jesus Christ!

You and I are on Earth to bring as many into the coming Kingdom as we possibly can! Our mission, like Jesus while He was on Earth, is not to condemn the world, but to save it through the message of the Kingdom. All the while displaying its dunamis power among the people of every nation, tongue and tribe, even to the ends of the Earth! We're not to just sit back and hold the fort until Jesus returns. Satan's the one trying to hold the fort. Why? Because the Church has been commissioned through Jesus to take his goods. Even Jesus said that the "gates of Hell" cannot hold up against the Church.

Remember "gates" are defensive, not offensive. Hell has gates to protect them from the attack of the Church!

When she comes into knowing her God given authority and power, nothing can stop her! Why do you think the devil works so hard at keeping the Church ignorant of the power? He knows that what you don't know you have, you will never use. However, if your reading this book, you're not ignorant any more are you? You've been commissioned and equipped to shake loose the Gates of Hell, and set free its captives!

You've been sent to set free those behind those gates, held captive to do the will of the evil one. You've been equipped to "trample upon ALL the power of the enemy" in Jesus Name! So what are you waiting for?

You might be wondering, "What does that look like?" That's a fair question considering that the present state of the Church provides us with few models. Let me share how I've walked in what we're talking about. And by the way I certainly haven't arrived when it comes to this, yet on the other hand, I'm not stepping out for the first time either. The point is that we all have to start somewhere.

One day my wife and I we're driving by a park and I saw a young man there who looked like he had a condition that stunted his growth. I knew this because his face looked as mature as the other boys at the park, yet he was only about 4 feet tall. The rest of the boys looked about 12-14 years old. Well after I saw him the Holy Spirit gripped my heart so intensely for me to go and minister to him. I must have driven around and circled the block five times in fear until finally I said, "Holy Spirit please fill me for this!" And guess what? He did! I felt a courage and boldness come over me almost instantly. Okay now I had no excuse! I knew this was God!

So I pulled the van over, and my son Judah and I got out together and went to speak with the boy. By the way, Judah asked if he could come, he loves to pray for people and anoint them with oil. If anyone ever even sneezes in our house, he wants to get the oil! I love it! It's just the culture we've created in our home. It's our biblical response, to natural consequence, in which we see supernatural benefit! So we walk over to the boy and ask him his name. He says, "My name is Brave Heart." We thought he was kidding at first, but a young girl with him who we later found out was his cousin said, "No really that's his name." I couldn't help it, I thought to myself, "Wow this has started out really positive already with a name like Brave Heart."We then proceeded to explain to him that we believe in God and His Son Jesus, and that God told to me to come pray for him.

Then we asked him if we could, and said that God would touch him in a special way. He said, "Sure!" with much enthusiasm! So we had him sit down and Judah and I laid hands on him and began praying. I have to admit, at this point I had full confidence that God would start growing his legs out right in front of us, but that's not what happened. Brave Heart began crying, quietly, but noticeably. I started praying harder, because his legs hadn't changed yet, but still no change in length.

We prayed for another while and then we closed and looked up at Brave Heart. He just starred at us with tears in his eyes and kept saying, "Thank you, thank you, thank you..." I'm thinking in my mind, "For what? Nothing happened!" Then his cousin spoke up, "No one ever really wants to come near Brave Heart, and some kids say that, 'He's just weird'. Then I finally got it! The miracle here was LOVE! Brave Heart felt the love of God and others that day like he had never before. As we left, he never stopped thanking us continually. I learned something that day that I'll never forget. We cannot overlook what we may not consider a miracle, for what we would consider grander happenings.

I shared this story first because we need to know and remember this even while reaching for the impossible! **"And now these three remain: faith, hope and love. But the greatest of these is LOVE." (1 Corinthians 13:13)**

Later on that same year we found out that a precious lady in our Church had collapsed in the local mall because her aorta had basically exploded! If you don't know, the Aorta is the largest artery in the body, beginning from the left ventricle of the heart. It circulates oxygenated blood to every part of the body throughout the body's system of circulation. That sounds important doesn't it? Well that's because it is!

We were told by many Doctors including the one who attends our Church, that she shouldn't even be alive today! But we prayed as "the Church" together. Remember "the Church", the force to be reckoned with? We got to praying that our God who binds up the broken hearted would bind up hers. We could only pray because she was immediately flown by helicopter to the nearest city which for us was a 4 1/2 hour drive away. But don't forget…

"the fervent prayer of the righteous is powerful and effective, and it accomplishes much!" (James 5:16)

We prayed that God would bind up her broken heart; He's in that business, if you didn't know. We prayed that He would guide the hands of the surgeons and He did! The surgery went without a hitch! They were able to surround and "bind up" her aorta with a mesh. However the interesting thing is that, to this day, they still can't seem to find the mesh when they view her in checkups! This to them remains a mystery, to us a miracle! However, even though the surgery was a success, she remained in a coma even after the anesthetics should have worn off. There was some warranted concern that she would not come out due to the trauma her body had just gone through. When we got the phone call, we got to praying again for her to awake and for full recovery. As my wife and I were praying together, I kept hearing deep in my heart, "Snap her out of it."

I thought, "That's weird" and kept on praying. Then again as I'm praying, "Snap her out of it!" this time it was louder! Okay, I knew this was God, so I spoke out of Christ in me and said, "In the name of Jesus Christ of Nazareth I command her to wake up." And I snapped my fingers as I said "wake up!" Now folks, this was an act of faith, I wasn't even near the city where she was.

Not even an hour after that we got a phone call, and they said, "She woke up about 45 minutes ago and she is doing amazing!" I mean come on! There is no way that was just a coincidence! That my friend was dynamite! Talk about a faith builder! I was ecstatic for her and her family first and foremost, and then for me, that God had used me powerfully in a such a simple act of faith.

You see, faith is the conduit in which the power of God flows.

Jesus always said to those who received miracles time and time again, "It was you're faith that healed you!" Remember what Peter and John had? Faith in the name of the Lord Jesus Christ! Remember the words of Jesus in John 14:12-14? He said, "**I tell you the truth, anyone who has faith in me will do what I have been doing. They will do even greater things than these, because I am going to the Father. And I will do whatever you ask in my name, so that the Son may bring glory to the Father. You may ask me for anything in my name, and I will do it.**" He will do what you ask in His name to bring glory to the father! That's the purpose. Jesus is very clear regarding us doing what he did for He said, "**I tell you the truth!**" so He was not lying. And He said "**anyone who has faith.**" There's no room for interpreting our way out of this one folks! For that matter, why would you want to? Yet to my amazement, some still try.

It really does amaze me how hard some theologians work at convincing the body of Christ that the power of God for His people has somehow left the premises. Or that it died with the Apostles. Have you ever heard that one? The problem is the Apostles weren't the only ones recorded doing miracles. Stephen for one, was not an Apostle, and God used him powerfully! Now his ministry was short to say the least, but still effective.

Jason Silver

The five-fold gifts of Apostle, Prophet, Evangelist, Pastor and Teacher were given by Christ to equip His Church for the work of the ministry. The last time I looked, the Church was still here, and so is a world in need of the ministry of the Church. Therefore we have not lost the need of these gifts for the equipping of the saints to do the work of ministry. **(See Ephesians 4:11-13)**

However it's like the Church has decided to turn the five-fold office gifts into the three-fold office gifts by only accepting the Evangelist, Pastor and Teacher. No one has problems with any of them. But when you start talking about the office gifts of Apostle and Prophet, well the majority of Church folks start to get nervous. Yet Ephesians chapter 4 gives absolutely no indication that the two office gifts just dropped off the wagon somewhere along the way. It really annoys me when you tell people you're thinking of attending Bible College, and they automatically say, "Oh, so you're going to be a Pastor." Folks... Pastor is not the only functioning gift in the Church. However, I could see why people would think this way. As far as I have seen, most Bible Colleges and Seminaries, do not seem to streamline their courses to any other office gift but the Pastor.

Or what about what we so confidently call "the Theologian"? This one really bugs me. Where is the Theologian even listed in the gifts that build up the Church? I guess we could fit it into Teacher somehow if they were actually teaching too. My point is this, how many Churches base what they believe in and do, on what the Theologians come up with? Many do, to say the least. So what's the problem with that? The problem is that it doesn't line up with our Early Church model at all. The Church is recorded in the Book of Acts as devoting themselves to "the Apostles" teaching! Not the Pastors, or the Evangelists, not the Teachers, and there is definitely no mention of anyone

92

consulting with what we would call "the theologian". Remember Paul said, **"My message and my preaching were not with wise and persuasive words, but with a demonstration of the Spirit's power, so that your faith might not rest on <u>men's wisdom</u>, but on <u>God's power</u>." (1 Corinthians 2:4-5)** So you be the judge, which one is Paul clearly saying our faith must rely on, "men's wisdom" or "God's power"? He's very clear that "God's power" is where our faith must lie. The Apostles were not some think tank of theology, they were practitioners of a new covenant life!

The question is where does the faith of the Church today primarily lie? Sadly it is mostly in the theologians', or men's wisdom. They were in Jesus day too; they were called the "teachers of the Law". They had the same problem then as many do today; they spent all their time studying and learning the Law yet never practicing it. Jesus once said of them that they were, "Ever learning, yet never perceiving." One thing that irritated "the teachers of the Law" about Jesus; was that He called them out, to do themselves the things that they were teaching others to do. And then He would demonstrate it by doing it Himself.

What really angered the teachers of the Law concerning Jesus, was that His lack of hypocrisy exposed their abundance of it!

It's kind of funny when you think about it. I realize that this may anger some, but I'm willing to take that risk, if the reward is to have an individual wake up to do what they have learned, and not just sit around and think about it. Unlike most folks, I tend to be unimpressed with any amount of letters of credential following an individual's name.

Not too unlike Paul when he said in Galatians 2:6, **"Whatever they were, it makes no difference to me; God shows personal favoritism to no man."** Our confidence must never be in the flesh, but in God.

We need to trust in God and what He says alone, not in what men can come up with. The driving point of this chapter is, that regardless of any accreditations by men, God has called each one of us who name Christ as Lord, to be carriers and releasers of His presence wherever we go. That really is what it means to minister. Ministry is giving God to people who do not have Him, and whether they know it or not, desperately need Him! God has given us His power to do this in the same manner that Jesus did.

Why would He equip Jesus to do a job, yet not equip us to do the same job? It's foolishness to think otherwise. Paul tells us that, **"God equips those whom He calls."** The church has been called and commissioned, so God therefore has, and is equipping her for "the work of the ministry". And He has chosen to equip her through the gifts of the Apostles, Prophets, Evangelists, Pastors and Teachers! So learn and release, learn and release, learn and release!

It really is that simple to understand that "Freely you have received, now freely give!" Just like the words to that older Vineyard song "Rain Down On Us" by Terry Butler, "We're vessels made to hold you glory, fill us up to overflowing, and pour us out on this thirsty world." Folks, this is our "Earth Purpose", it's why we're still here, and also why we weren't raptured at the moment of salvation. We need to remember this.

CHAPTER 5
Waiting for an Elijah

"See, I will send you the prophet Elijah before that great and awesome day of the Lord comes.
Malachi 4:5-6

Elijah was regarded as one of Israel's greatest prophets. He changed weather patterns over Israel, raised the dead, called down fire from heaven multiple times, and was taken up to heaven in a whirlwind, avoiding the experience of a normal physical death. Some of my favorite records in the Bible are of Elijah and Elisha. Elijah was so great in fact, that at Jesus' transfiguration, **"...there appeared before them Elijah and Moses, who were talking with Jesus."** [Mark 9:4]

The Jews hang onto the promise of Elijah's return and wait patiently for him, even to this day. In addition to this, the Jewish Passover meal to this day includes a place set for Elijah, in hopes of his return. The problem is, waiting for him is pointless. Elijah returned in bodily form in John the Baptist. We are told this by Jesus Himself. Elijah is not expected back again. We now await Jesus' return as our Savior at the end of the age, but biblically, Elijah's return has come and gone.

Back in 1998 I remember asking the Lord, "God, please send me an Elijah!" What I meant was, someone who truly operated in the power of God, that I could learn from. Not to mention there was also at the time a teaching going around on what we today call "mentoring". The whole point of the teaching was that we needed to be like Elisha, and find an Elijah. Even though Elijah actually found Elisha. What was meant by "an Elijah" was someone more mature and experienced in the things of God than we were. Really it was about finding someone to disciple you.

God let me pray that for months, and yet my Elijah never seemed to surface. So I asked God with even more fervor, thinking maybe that would get me an answer. Well it did, but not the one I expected. As I was asking for God to send me an Elijah for what would be the last time, He spoke this loudly in my heart, "You be an Elijah!" I was like "What?" And then He said, "Don't wait for someone else to do what I called you to do, now rise up and do it!" Wow! What a revelation that was! I was like "Yeah! Why wait around for someone else when God has equipped me to do the impossible if I but believe!" You see, I wasn't taught it, I caught it!

After being involved in ministry now for many years, I find this to be the mentality in the Church. It's like everyone is waiting for the one anointed man or woman of God that God will use to heal, deliver, or change them. We want to leave the sacrifices involved in becoming a diligent servant of God to someone else, and simply share in their reward when they get it for their own due diligence in seeking God.

I believe that this is a part of what Jesus was expressing when He said, **"The harvest is plentiful, but the workers are few. Ask the Lord of the harvest, therefore, to send out workers into his harvest field."** And then He says to His disciples, **"Go! I am sending you…" (Luke 10:2-3)** This is still what Jesus is saying to the Church today, "GO". Church, let's stop waiting for someone else to come along and do it, let us do it!

LET THE WEAK SAY "I AM STRONG."

According to Kingdom standards, if you think that you're inadequate, if you think you may not be qualified or even make the cut, then you're actually perfect for the job!

My goodness just look at the story of Gideon.

"Now the Angel of the Lord came and sat under the terebinth tree which was in Ophrah, which belonged to Joash the Abiezrite, while his son Gideon threshed wheat in the winepress, in order to hide it from the Midianites. And the Angel of the Lord appeared to him, and said to him, "The Lord is with you, you mighty man of valor!" (Judges 6:11-12) What?! Are you kidding me? Mighty man of valor? The dude was hiding in a wine press! Yet God saw him as mighty!

"But sir," Gideon replied, "if the Lord is with us, why has all this happened to us? Where are all his wonders that our fathers told us about when they said, 'Did not the Lord bring us up out of Egypt?' But now the Lord has abandoned us and put us into the hand of

Midian." The Lord turned to him and said, "Go in the strength you have and save Israel out of Midian's hand. Am I not sending you?" "But Lord," Gideon asked, "how can I save Israel? My clan is the weakest in Manasseh, and I am the least in my family." (Judges 6:13-15)

Wow! Yet two more seemingly valid reasons why Gideon may not be the man for the job; his clan was the weakest in the land, and he was the weakest in his family. Surely God could not use this sad excuse of a man could He? Did you notice that Gideon mentions the wonders done through Moses in Egypt? He was wondering where his Elijah was. Or in this case, Moses. The same principle at work.

Gideon was waiting for someone else to do it, for someone else to come to their rescue. That is until God came and said, "You do it!" It really is hard to believe that Gideon was God's chosen man, when you read on further and find out he still doubts God two more times with the fleece. Yet as weak and full of doubt as Gideon was, God chose him. And obviously God knew what He was doing, for this was the result:

"Gideon and the hundred men with him reached the edge of the camp at the beginning of the middle watch, just after they had changed the guard. They blew their trumpets and broke the jars that were in their hands. The three companies blew the trumpets and smashed the jars. Grasping the torches in their left hands and holding in their right hands the trumpets they were to blow, they shouted, "A sword for the Lord and for Gideon!"

While each man held his position around the camp, all the Midianites ran, crying out as they fled. When the three hundred trumpets sounded, the Lord caused the men throughout the camp to turn on each other with their swords." (Judges 7:19-22)

A SIMPLE SHEPHERD BOY

"Samuel asked Jesse, "Are these all the sons you have?""There is still the youngest," Jesse answered, "but he is tending the sheep." Samuel said, "Send for him; we will not sit down until he arrives." So he sent and had him brought in. He was ruddy, with a fine appearance and handsome features. Then the Lord said, "Rise and anoint him; he is the one."

So Samuel took the horn of oil and anointed him in the presence of his brothers, and from that day on the Spirit of the Lord came upon David in power." (1 Samuel 16:11-13)

Here we find David, a simple shepherd boy, most likely reeking of sheep, manure, and the fields, not to mention the youngest and most inexperienced in his family, being chosen by God to be King! How can this be. Even Samuel, the great prophet, who "heard God" didn't see it coming! **"Samuel saw Eliab and thought, "Surely the Lord's anointed stands here before the Lord." But the Lord said to Samuel, "Do not consider his appearance or his height, for I have rejected him. The Lord does not look at the things man looks at. Man looks at the outward appearance, but the Lord looks at the heart.""** (1 Samuel 16:6-7)

Now David was the opposite of Gideon, in that he wasn't the type to sit back and wait for someone else to do something, he would just do it! Most of us know the account of David and Goliath by now. As the story goes, Saul and the armies of Israel simply sat back in fear at the ranting of one giant uncircumcised Philistine named Goliath. What were they waiting for? Someone else to do something of course! Yet while a whole army sat back in fear, one young boy experienced only in killing a few wild animals, stood up against a giant in the Name of the Lord! Yes, one too young, too weak in stature, and inexperienced in battle boy put a whole army to shame! He wasn't waiting for an Elijah, he became one!

UNEDUCATED & UNTRAINED MEN

"Now when they saw the boldness of Peter and John, and perceived that they were uneducated and untrained men, they marveled. And they realized that they had been with Jesus . And seeing the man who had been healed standing with them, they could say nothing against it.

But when they had commanded them to go aside out of the council, they conferred among themselves, saying, "What shall we do to these men?

For, indeed, that a notable miracle has been done through them is evident to all who dwell in Jerusalem, and we cannot deny it. (Acts 4:13-17)

You see unlike the world, and the church that can sometimes be worldly, God has different standards and qualifications when he chooses people to do His work, and represent His Kingdom. I mean, if we would but for a minute compare our standards for an individual to be able to minister, to God's standards; we would be in for quite a surprise indeed! It may sound funny at first, but when I did this very thing in my own ministry, I realized I actually had to lower my standards! I always struggled trying to do everything myself and became resentful towards it in the meantime. Who knew that I was actually causing my own grief. My standards were too high to release anyone to do anything.

Look at the yahoos Jesus picked, I mean really! They made Him look bad all the time, they struggled to believe in and trust Him, they stole money from Him (Judas), and they weren't trained at all to do anything to do with ministry! Does this sound like your short list of potential leaders? Yet God chose them! Jesus said, **"Those whom You gave Me I have kept; and none of them is lost except the son of perdition..." (John 17:12)** They were handpicked by God, for Jesus' ministry team. After Jesus went back to the Father, the disciples, now Apostles, continued on the work of Jesus. Jesus taught them to do the stuff, He never taught them to wait for Elijah to come do it.

THE CLERGY AND LAYMEN DILEMMA

"It was he who gave some to be apostles, some to be prophets, some to be evangelists, and some to be pastors and teachers, to prepare God's people for works of ministry, so that the body of Christ may be built up until

we all reach unity in the faith and in the knowledge of the Son of God and become mature, attaining to the whole measure of the fullness of Christ.

Then we will no longer be infants, tossed back and forth by the waves, and blown here and there by every wind of teaching and by the cunning and craftiness of men in their deceitful scheming. Instead, speaking the truth in love, we will in all things grow up into him who is the Head, that is, Christ. From him the whole body, joined and held together by every supporting ligament, grows and builds itself up in love, <u>as each part does its work.</u>" (Ephesians 4:11-16)

In many Churches today a distinction is made between those who are "clergy" and those who are "laity". "At the beginning of the Church, most of the work of the congregation was done by people who had no official position. It was people simply wanting to serve as Jesus taught them. Their efforts therefore were offered out of a heart to serve. However by the middle of the third century, it shifted, and the work was only to be done by the professional clergy. Unfortunately, this has created an unbiblical, and unhealthy mentality in the Church of today.

In thinking this way "Well the Pastor does it all, because we pay him." The majority of the Church (the people) avoid responsibility in carrying out any type of ministry. They simply watch the Pastor, or the leaders do it all. And they're fine with that. That is until leadership does something they don't like, or agree with, and then they proceed to complain, and instruct leadership on how it should be done. I've always wondered exactly, just what personal experience they're basing their instruction on? What I mean is, it amazes me how many people know what a Pastor should, and should not be doing, even though they have NEVER actually Pastored before.

Anyone who becomes a believer in Jesus Christ *has* entered the ministry. The Bible does not speak of the Christian, who is not also a minister in some way. It's simple; if you believe, then you're a minster. Not all will walk in the Five-Fold gifts, but all should walk in something. Let that sink in for a bit, and you'll probably have to, because we have been told differently for so long. Didn't Jesus say in Mark 16:17-18, **"And these signs will accompany <u>those who believe</u>: In my name they will drive out demons; they will speak in new tongues; they will pick up snakes with their hands; and when they drink deadly poison, it will not hurt them at all; they will place their hands on sick people, and they will get well."**

Folks, all these signs are ministry. Notice Jesus didn't say, "And these signs will follow those who are trained, and qualified, and meet the standard."? No.

The only training and qualification needed is to BELIEVE! Just believe!

I make a point in the Church I Pastor to always exhort my people to minster in whatever way they can. I intentionally downplay the Clergy/Laity mindset as much as I can and encourage an "Every Member a Minister" attitude whenever I have the opportunity. I think some ministers may be afraid to do this because they feel they will lose respect as the Pastor from their people. But in my experience that has not been the case at all. Remember Ephesians 4:11? We who are of a particular ministry calling such as Pastor and Teacher are called, "...**to prepare God's people for works of ministry...**"

Part of that, is first helping them to understand that they are indeed called to minister. I tell my Church, "Don't wait to pray for someone who's sick until the Pastor arrives, you pray!" "Don't run around the Church building after the service trying to find the Pastor to meet a ministry need... you meet it!" I've seen people look really put off by this, but according to my Biblical job description, it's really what I'm supposed to be doing. Listen, if you're a Pastor reading this book, I'm telling you the truth. If you don't empower your people to do the work, then they'll always look to you to do it for them. They will always be waiting for an Elijah.

WHY JESUS HAD TO GO

If Jesus never left Earth, the disciples would have continually looked to Him to get the job done.

So He had to leave them, but He left them fully equipped. **"But I tell you the truth: It is for your good that I am going away. Unless I go away, the Counselor will not come to you; but if I go, I will send him to you." (John 16:7-8)**

"On one occasion, while he was eating with them, he gave them this command: "Do not leave Jerusalem, but wait for the gift my Father promised, which you have heard me speak about. For John baptized with water, but in a few days you will be baptized with the Holy Spirit and power." (Acts 1:4-5) Jesus tells the disciples, "It's good that I go away." Why did He say this? They we're probably thinking, "No Jesus! It would be good if you could stay!" But Jesus told them it was good, because then they would receive the Holy Spirit and power! Power for what? Power to minister like Jesus, who was anointed with the Holy Spirit and power, and went around doing good!

My main point here however, is that if Jesus never left, then the disciples would have continually looked to Him to do things, rather than take responsibility to do it themselves. I have found that one of the most important aspects of being a Leader is to learn to leave people alone. What I mean is, once you show someone the way to do something, then get out of the way. If you don't then they will continue to look to you to lead instead of them taking responsibility to do the leading themselves.

When I ask someone to lead a ministry, I usually will not attend the meeting on purpose, because if I'm there as "the Pastor", everyone looks to me instead of their new ministry leader. It really does lead to confusion, and decreases the effectiveness of that ministry time. Many leaders who like to have "all their ducks in a row" struggle with this idea. But if they want to avoid "burnout" they will eventually need to put it into practice.

PASSING THE BATON

I do not think a coincidence that just like Elijah was taken up to Heaven in the sight of Elisha, Jesus was taken up to Heaven in the sight of His disciples. And just as Elijah left his mantle for Elisha in the process, so Jesus left His for His Church.

Ephesians 4:7-13 says…

"But to each one of us grace has been given as Christ apportioned it. This is why it says: "When he <u>ascended on high</u>, he led captives in his train and <u>gave gifts to men</u> ." What does "he ascended" mean except that he also descended to the lower, earthly regions? He who descended is the very one who ascended higher than all the heavens, in order to fill the whole universe.

It was he who gave some to be apostles, some to be prophets, some to be evangelists, and some to be pastors and teachers, to prepare God's people for works of service, so that the body of Christ may be built up until we all reach unity in the faith and in the knowledge of the Son of

God and become mature, attaining to the whole measure of the fullness of Christ."

These gifts, or mantle's, given by Christ have become known in theological circles as the Five Fold Ministry. They are gifts from Jesus to the Church! They are not meant only to benefit the individuals who are called to walk in them, but are to benefit the Church. Apostles, Prophets, Evangelists, Pastors and Teachers are given by Jesus to train His Church around the world to "DO MINISTRY". They were not given to do *all* the work for the Church.

"As they were walking along and talking together, suddenly a chariot of fire and horses of fire appeared and separated the two of them, and Elijah went up to heaven in a whirlwind. Elisha saw this and cried out, "My father! My father! The chariots and horsemen of Israel!" And Elisha saw him no more. Then he took hold of his own clothes and tore them apart.

He picked up the cloak that had fallen from Elijah and went back and stood on the bank of the Jordan. 14 Then he took the cloak that had fallen from him and struck the water with it. "Where now is the Lord, the God of Elijah?" he asked. When he struck the water, it divided to the right and to the left, and he crossed over." (2 Kings 2:11-14)

It's quite obvious that just like Elisha walked away from the fiery chariot experience with the same power and spirit that Elijah walked, the Church has been given the Five Fold ministry, and the Holy Spirit's power to walk in the same way Jesus did! So following the logic here, we could rightly say that Jesus was our Elijah. He's come, and gone back to the Father. And He has left His mantle for His Church. Don't get me wrong, Jesus was much greater than Elijah, but you get the point.

YOU HAVE TO A...S...K TO G...E...T

A friend of mine once said, as he listened to me whine about not having a particular thing in my life, "Jason, you have to A...S...K to G...E...T." At first it sounds selfish, but asking to get something is not selfish, if it's with the right motive. Even Jesus said, **"Ask and it will be given to you; seek and you will find; knock and the door will be opened to you. For everyone who asks receives; he who seeks finds; and to him who knocks, the door will be opened."**

"Which of you, if his son asks for bread, will give him a stone? Or if he asks for a fish, will give him a snake? If you, then, though you are evil, know how to give good gifts to your children, how much more will your Father in heaven give good gifts to those who ask him!" (Matthew 7:7-12)

For us to go without things may appear spiritual, but Jesus was the most spiritual man to walk the Earth; and He tells us to ask for what we need!

As I mentioned earlier on, it would be unreasonable for Jesus to leave us to continue on His work, yet without the tools that He used. It was the Father's plan all along to have Jesus pass his toolkit to His Church. The tools really are available to **"all who believe"** and to all **"who ask Him."** We've been told differently in many Church circles, but if I can be completely honest, it's a lie! I know this, firstly from what the Word says, and secondly, from my own personal experience. (Note the order: Bible first. Experience second) When I sought the **"baptism of the Holy Spirit"**(Matthew 1:7-8)or to be "**clothed in power from in high"** (Luke 24:49) and asked for **"the promise of the Father"**(Acts 1:1-8) the Holy Spirit and Power, I received Him!

The Bible is VERY clear that God will give this person and power of the Holy Spirit to those WHO ASK. You see how the devil has duped the Church? So, if He can get the Church to believe that the power isn't for today, then they won't bother asking. The last thing the devil needs, is you and I running around in the same power as Jesus, and destroying all the sinful works he's accomplished on this Earth! I mean if I was him, I would follow the same battle plan which is: keep the Church ignorant of the power that makes her effective. So Jesus has passed the baton, but few are taking it. Most because they are ignorant to the fact that there is one, and some who just don't want to take it.

I remember hearing a gentleman say once, "Well if God wants me to have this supposed baptism in the Holy Spirit, then He'll just give it to me." And many people have based their belief system on this line of thinking. I really thought about what he said. We know and believe that God wants everyone to be saved, and He has provided a way, but people still have to ASK. God doesn't just save people out of the blue, while their walking down the street one day. No, they have to hear the message concerning the gift, believe the message, and then ask to receive the gift for themselves. The baptism in the Holy Spirit is also a gift. So then, why would it be any different? So then God does want you to have it, but you still have to lay down your pride and ask. Remember what Jesus Himself said, **"...your Father in heaven will give good gifts to those who ask him!" (Matthew 7:12)**

WIDESPREAD BIBLICAL ILLITERACY

I've never understood why so many Christians will say "The Word of God is everything I stand on." Yet a majority of believers don't even know what the Bible really teaches or says regarding God and life.

And that's because the only time they blow the dust off and crack it open, is on Sunday mornings. And some folks don't even bring their Bibles to Church anymore. Remember what I talked about earlier, Jesus told us to pray, **"Give us THIS DAY our DAILY BREAD."** He never said to pray, "Give us on SUNDAY or ONE DAY bread." Jesus also said, **"For man does not live on bread alone, but on EVERY WORD that proceeds from the mouth of God"** It sounds like Jesus is saying we can't really live without it. I believe that is what He's saying.

Of course one could say, "Well I'm not in my Bible much at all, but I'm still alive." And my question would be "Are you *REALLY* alive?" You may think your sustained, but inside, your spirit is emaciated and weak, and you probably lack the faith to pray for a flea. Don't believe me? Romans 10:17 says, **"Faith comes by hearing, and hearing by the word of God."** In light of this truth, logic would say; the more Word of God that **you** hear, the more faith you will walk in. And let's not forget that, **"Without faith it is impossible to please God, because anyone who comes to him must believe that he exists and that he rewards those who earnestly seek him. (Hebrew 11:6)**

In my own experience growing up in the Church in various denominations (both Evangelical & Pentecostal) I've noticed that we tend to live off of other people's faith instead of our own. Which certainly doesn't help our current "Clergy and Laymen Dilemma." We don't bother to seek God on our own, when we can easily run to the Pastor to pray for us, or give us counsel, or answers. I will intentionally not answer a lot of biblical questions that people ask me. Of course not without telling them to look into for themselves. If I answer every person's question about the Bible, then I am actually enabling them to not have to get into it for themselves.

Remember, the purpose of this chapter is to encourage people to stop waiting for a man or woman of God, and to actually become one themselves.

2 Timothy 2:15 says...

"Study to show yourself approved unto God, a workman that needs not to be ashamed, but rightly divides the word of God."

However, we cannot truly be a man or a woman of God, if we don't really know God. We get to know God just like we do anyone else. In any relationship, we get to know someone by what they reveal about themselves in what they *say*. Their words reveal who they are.

Matthew 12:34 says...

"For out of the abundance of a man's heart his mouth speaks."

Your heart (or your spirit) is the real you. That's why God, like when choosing David as King, doesn't look at the outside of a man, but looks at the heart. On the outside we can put up a front, and appear different than we really are to other people. But we cannot put up a front in our hearts.

Seeing that God has nothing to hide, He never puts up a front, but always speaks from His heart. The Bible is the revealed heart of God to mankind. I don't get to know God through an experience, although they help, I get to know God through His word. This is why the prophets of old "knew God" better than others, because He spoke to them, and they heard His words. We don't have to wait for a prophet to come to town anymore, to hear from God, we've been given His Word. The Bible comes in so many media formats nowadays, that we really have no excuse not to read it, listen to it, or watch it. So the only reason I can see, is people just don't want to.

In my estimation, there's a real incongruency with many Christians saying they love God, but at the same time, they rarely want to hear from Him. If I treated my wife that way, I'm quite certain she would doubt my love for her. And she would have every right to for that matter.

In saying all of this, I want you to understand something. It's not so much that we need to get into the Word of God, as much as we need to get the Word in us. A mature believer should have a stockpile, as it were, of God's word in their hearts. What happens in times of crisis, when you do not have a physical Bible in hand? You should not be like a fish out of water. You should have enough Word of God in you, to speak to that crisis. Jesus and the disciples never carried scrolls around everywhere so they could use them as a reference when need be. No, the Word of God was in their hearts, and on their lips. Jesus knew God the Father, and the disciples knew Jesus. They knew what the Father would do in any situation and they did it too. How? Out of relationship.

IGNORANCE CREATES BAD DOCTRINE

Unfortunately, biblical ignorance is also the main reason for bad doctrines in the Church today. People tend to form what they think to be concrete beliefs, from little actual biblical knowledge. I've also found that many people I've talked to over the years, form what they believe from what "so and so" said in their book, tapes, or sermons. The problem is that their doctrine is based off of a conglomerate of what everyone else has said, rather than what they got out of their Bible for themselves.

The problem with this, is that it's not their own belief, it's someone else's. If you don't really own a belief system, it won't hold you through the tough times in this life. Even

Jesus knowing what others were saying about Him asked Peter in Matthew 16:16-17, **"Who do you say that I am?" Peter answered, "You are the Christ, the Son of the living God." Jesus replied, "Blessed are you, Simon son of Jonah, for this was not revealed to you by man, but by my Father in heaven.**

You see, Peter believed because of his own revelation given to him by God. Listen, if what you have has been given to you by men, then men can take it away. However, if what you have has been given by God, then no man can take it away. God hasn't chosen to build His Church upon the ideas and philosophies of men, rather upon the true revelation knowledge of Him, given by Him. I don't care if you have doctorates in divinity coming out your ears, if you still haven't gotten a revelation from God, regarding who He really is; you're supposed education was a waste of time and money.

BREAK THE CYCLE : A WORD TO CHURCH LEADERS

According to what we read earlier in Ephesians Chapter 4, the responsibility to train the Church to do the work is ours.

As leaders, we need to intentionally break the spectator cycle in our Churches through the way that we lead.

There's an unspoken rule that's tends to be very prominent in many Churches. It's called "the 80/20 Rule." You may have heard of it. It means that 80% of the people in the Church sit and watch, while 20% do the work. Now, the percentages may vary slightly in different congregations, but from the cross section of Churches I've been in, it's not by much.

We need to empower people to do something, rather than enable them to do nothing. As I mentioned earlier, the whole "clergy/laymen" thought pattern is essentially to blame for this. However, the only reason we even have this mentality is because that's what people have always been taught. All we as leaders have to do is re-teach. We need to intentionally cause a paradigm shift in the Church through the way we lead people. We cannot expect it to happen, if it's not coming from Church leadership.

It's going to take us Church leaders laying aside our fears and inhibitions of releasing others to do what we do, and not be concerned about our own personal job security.

When it comes right down to it, Pastoring is not a job anyways, it's a calling.

A WORD TO THE FLOCK

"Remember your leaders , who spoke the word of God to you. Consider the outcome of their way of life and imitate their faith." (Hebrews 13:7)

"Obey your leaders and submit to their authority. They keep watch over you as men who must give an account. Obey them so that their work will be a joy, not a burden, for that would be of no advantage to you." (Hebrews 13:17)

On average I find most folks in the Church really don't like change at all. We as human beings tend to cling to predictability. It gives us a sense of security. Albeit, this very sense, can be a false one at best. Yet it is change, and even taking risks, that cause us as people, and as the Church to progress and mature. So I encourage you to be open to change when it comes through your leadership. It's not easy for leaders to make vital changes in the Church.

Overall we as leaders want people to be happy, but if we are truly godly, people's happiness will never be at the cost of disobeying God. We can make it easier for our leaders, by showing our support and submission to the authority of their God-given calling and appointment in the Church. When we link arms with our leaders, imitate their faith, and get behind their vision, we will also share in their rewards.

CHAPTER 6
The Road Ahead

"But the people who know their God will be strong, and will perform great exploits."

Daniel 11:32-33

The Bible is very clear that these last days will grow darker and darker before the return of Christ. And that the world will become as wicked as in the days of Noah. However, as the world grows darker, the Church will grow brighter! Remember, Jesus told us that we are the light of the world! **"Greater is He that's in us, than he that is the world."** You see the world getting darker is actually an opportunity for the Church. Why? When everything gets dark what's the first thing people look for? A light! If you go out in a boat at night and shine a bright light into the water, fish will gather to the light.

There's something attractive about light, light makes us feel safe, light makes things clear and visible.

This is why I have an issue with hard lined "seeker models" of doing Church. That is: *a purposeful sensitivity to in no way offend, or conflict with people, as to not lose favor with them.* In other words; Church leaders try to make their Church services look just like the world, so as not to offend anyone that may come to their service.

The problem is, the seeker is actually looking for something different than what they currently have, otherwise they wouldn't be seeking for something else in the first place. So the "seeker model" ends up working against itself in the end. I'm not talking about being relevant; I believe we need to communicate to a generation in a manner that they actually understand. Paul spoke of relevancy when he said, **"I'll become all things to all men, that I might save some."** However, he didn't dim the gospel light; he simply let it shine in a way that the culture he was speaking to understood. And he also did not sin, so he could reach the sinner.

As matter of fact, the one thing I love about the Bible, is that it's never irrelevant. The Bible has answers to many questions and principles to live life by that never lose their relevancy. Wanting to have righteousness, peace and joy in our lives is just as relevant today, as it was in 1847, or even 76AD. So I do not believe for one minute that the seeker model Church is where God is taking us on the road ahead. In fact the only model fit to be considered, is the church as recorded in the Book of Acts. Why? Because it's in the Bible! In power is how we the Church were started, it's how we should continue, it is how we must finish! There's no place in scripture that references the Church as a weak, useless, powerless institution. So for us to behave in this manner, is unbiblical and quite frankly unacceptable!

I believe with all my heart that these last days will be like the Days of Elijah again. That the Church will once again operate in Gods divine supernatural ability! That we will speak once again as ones having authority, because we WILL actually use the authority we've been given! People will fear us because of what God is doing through us! People will once again begin to take the Church seriously, and many will be added to our numbers daily by the Spirit of God! This is the Church I see on the road that lies ahead.

However, this Church can only be established, if we are willing to leave what's not of it, on the road behind us. If we're to honest about it, this is the part most people struggle with. Leaving the things behind that aren't working seems to be very hard for people to do. I've personally never understood this. In my own thinking, it's like, "If what you're doing isn't working, then why are you doing it?" You need to do something else.

It seems to be human nature that we get comfortable with what's familiar, so much so, that we don't seem to care if what we're doing even works or not. But just because it's familiar and predictable, we take comfort in it. I'm convinced that Jesus came to comfort the disturbed, and to disturb those in comfort. The Pharisees for example, had quite a comfy system going on until Jesus showed up on the scene. Then all of a sudden they started to get a little uncomfortable. He did things different, and they didn't like that at all. But the way He did things wasn't just different, it was right. So we aren't only looking to do things different, but to do them right.

And if you want to do anything right, it's always best to refer back to the Manual. This is why I believe strongly in the Church getting back to, and growing out of its roots clearly laid out in the Bible. I believe the Book of Acts is the clearest reference we have as to what the life and purpose of the Church should look like. I don't care how good someone else's book on Church life and purpose is, if it doesn't reference the Book of Acts, then it is severely lacking.

PERSECUTION COMING TO NORTH AMERICA

"If the world hates you, keep in mind that it hated me first. If you belonged to the world, it would love you as its

own. As it is, you do not belong to the world, but I have chosen you out of the world. That is why the world hates you. Remember the words I spoke to you: 'No servant is greater than his master.' If they persecuted me, they will persecute you also. If they obeyed my teaching, they will obey yours also. They will treat you this way because of my name, for they do not know the One who sent me." John 15:18-21

The North American Church in general has enjoyed much religious freedom over many years, but this will change in the very near future. Things are already heating up against the Church and true Christianity. And especially as the church becomes more like Christ in action, the spirit of antichrist will rise against it even more. The word Christ means the anointed One, and His anointing, so antichrist actually means against the Christ and His anointing.

When the Church once again begins to operate in the anointing given to us by Jesus, there will be guaranteed opposition. That's why Jesus told us that, **"The servant is no greater than the master. If they persecute me they will also persecute you."** You'd have to be blind not to notice that the same world that demands us to be tolerant of it, is quickly growing more and more intolerant of us. However if we Christians truly understood the reason for persecution, we wouldn't view it so negatively.

For example in Matthew 5:11-12 Jesus tells us that "**Blessed are you when people insult you, persecute you and falsely say all kinds of evil against you because of Me. Rejoice and be glad, because great is your reward in heaven, for in the same way they persecuted the prophets who were before you.**" When we are persecuted because of Jesus, it's a good thing! When we identify ourselves with Christ to the point that we share in His sufferings, the Father also causes us to share in Christ's reward!

The Church in the Book of Acts understood this. In Acts 5:41 it says, **"The apostles left the Sanhedrin, <u>rejoicing</u> because they had been counted worthy of suffering disgrace for the sake of the Name."** You see they knew that if you were persecuted for doing what was right, then you were on the right track with God! Remember Jesus only did what was right and good, and for this they crucified Him!

1 Peter 4:14-16 says, **"If you are insulted because of the name of Christ, you are blessed, for the Spirit of glory and of God rests on you. If you suffer, it should not be as a murderer or thief or any other kind of criminal, or even as a troublemaker. However, if you suffer as a Christian, do not be ashamed, but praise God that you bear that His name."** And then Peter says in 1 Peter 2:20-21, **"But how is it to your credit if you receive a beating for doing wrong and endure it? But if you suffer for doing good and you endure it, this is commendable before God. <u>To this you were called</u>, because Christ suffered for you, leaving you an example that you should follow in his steps."**

You see persecution for the sake of Jesus name actually gives us confidence before God that we are on the right track! Persecution is an indication of right and holy living! Paul gives us this promise in 2 Timothy 3:11-13 when he says, **"In fact, everyone who wants to live a godly life in Christ Jesus will be persecuted."** It's simple to understand really, if you start to live like Jesus, you will most certainly end up being treated the same as Jesus was. However, like I said earlier, if we truly understand the principle of the matter, that God's righteousness is the cause of the persecution, then we will rejoice in it!

We can confidently rejoice in that we must be doing what Jesus did, because what happened to Him is now happening to us! We know that Paul the Apostle understood and walked in this himself when He said in Colossians 1:24-25,

"I rejoice in what I suffered for your sake, and I fill up in my flesh what is still lacking in regard to Christ's afflictions, for the sake of his body, which is the church." Basically, Paul was saying that he had suffered persecution in bringing the Gospel to the Church in Colossae, but not yet to the degree that Christ had suffered it in bringing us life.

I know that persecution never sounds like an encouraging subject. However, understanding the reason behind it, will help us walk in and through it with joy and hope of a great and lasting reward from God our Father! It will help us press on towards the heavenly stored prize that awaits us when the Kingdom comes to the New Earth which God will give us!

When Heaven meets Earth, we will finally know and see what all of this was for.

And all the mysteries that remain, will be revealed in the very instant that we see the face of Jesus, our God, and King! When we see Him as He now is, and become what we have longed to be... just like Him!

I love how Paul encourages us concerning this in 2 Corinthians 4:16-18 when he says, **"Therefore we do not lose heart. Though outwardly we are wasting away, yet inwardly we are being renewed day by day. Our light and momentary troubles are achieving for us an eternal glory that far outweighs them all. So we fix our eyes not on what is seen, but on what is unseen. For what is seen is temporary, but what is unseen is eternal."** Whenever my loving wife sees me stressing over anything, she always asks me, "What difference does this make in all of eternity Jason?"

It's amazing how quickly an eternal perspective, will bring into focus, a temporary one. We as the Church need to maintain an eternal perspective. The reason for this, is that, the future before us holds eternal reward for what we do in this temporary life. We are living for eternity, what we're in now is a temporary age, it's going to end, a new eternal age is coming, so why in the world would I put all my effort into living for this temporary one if it's not going to last?

When it comes down to it, it's just like investing; everyone is looking for the stock that has the best long-term pay out. The commodity of this present life is failing to make room for the next one that will **"never perish, spoil, or fade." (1 Peter 1:4)** The scripture says in Hebrews 12:2 that Jesus was able to endure the cross because of the joy set before Him.

So because Jesus knew all those who would be eternally saved, healed and delivered through His sacrifice on the cross, it helped Him to endure it! Jesus worldview was not temporary but eternal! Jesus tells us in Revelation 22:12 that, **"Behold, I am coming soon! My reward is with me, and I will give to everyone according to what he has done."** Notice He says, "My reward..." we share in Jesus reward! Immeasurable riches, unfading glory, everlasting joy and peace, and all this in the presence of God and Father forever and ever! Amen.

We must keep this as our focus and destination on the journey ahead of us! It will keep us on track, and in line with God's purpose for our lives! Paul makes this incredibly clear in Philippians 3:12-15 when he says, **"Not that I have already obtained all this, or have already been made perfect, but I press on to take hold of that for which Christ Jesus took hold of me. Brothers, I do not consider myself yet to have taken hold of it. But one thing I do: Forgetting what is behind and straining toward what is ahead, I press on toward the goal to win the prize for which God has called me heavenward in Christ Jesus. All of us who are mature should take such a view of things."** What view of things? An eternal one!

He reiterates this in Colossians 3:1-2 saying, **"Since, then, you have been raised with Christ, set your hearts on things above, where Christ is seated at the right hand of God. Set your minds on things above, not on earthly things."** God desires that His people live like the kingdom now, in order to gain the kingdom to come.

We are citizens of the coming heavenly kingdom, we're not of this worlds ways. The Bible is clear we're living for heaven come to earth; Jesus said that, **"The meek will inherit the earth."** He told us to pray, **"Let your kingdom COME, let your will be done on earth as it is done in heaven."** This is why we are to set our minds on things above, because one day, in God's time, the things above will come down and change all the things below!

John tells us this in vivid detail in Revelation 21:1-4 when he says, **"Then I saw a new heaven and a new earth, for the first heaven and the first earth had passed away, and there was no longer any sea. I saw the Holy City, the New Jerusalem, <u>coming down out of heaven</u> from God, prepared as a bride beautifully dressed for her husband. And I heard a loud voice from the throne saying, "Now the dwelling of God is with men, and he will live with them. They will be his people, and God himself will be with them and be their God. He will wipe every tear from their eyes. There will be no more death or mourning or crying or pain, for the old order of things has passed away."**

Folks this is "the joy set before us" with which we will be able to endure the road ahead of us. When we see the destination before us, we will be prepared for the road to get there! Our perspective should and must be the kingdom of God. This is why Jesus preached the Kingdom; it's what we're living for. It's the eternal destination of this temporary journey! Why do you think Jesus told people to do whatever they could, and pay whatever cost they had to, to gain the Kingdom? Because it's everything!

The Church needs to get back to this perspective, everything we say and do needs to come out of this kingdom reality.

This means that if the things we're doing do not serve the mandate of the kingdom of God, then we need to let them go, period. If they do not serve kingdom purpose; then they're a waste of time. Everything Jesus did on Earth was rooted in, and done out of Kingdom purpose. When we reach out to people, it must be for the purpose of getting them into the Kingdom. When we gather as the Church, it should be in encouragement and hope of the coming Kingdom. The point is this: If the destination is the Kingdom, then we should only follow the road that leads to it! Any other road will not get us there. If you're planning on going to Hawaii, you're not going to board a plane going to Iceland. It really is that simple.

SO WHAT HAPPENS WHEN NOTHING HAPPENS?

This is probably the question that most people struggle with when it comes to this journey of faith… What if nothing happens? What if a person doesn't get healed? What if they don't receive Christ? I think this is the best way to conclude this book. I've met many people that have been disappointed with the whole Pentecostal and Charismatic movement. They we're taught to "Just believe God, and you will see Him perform His promise" and then when either nothing happened or something happened differently than they thought it would, they were left feeling disappointed with God, and with the people who taught them.

I think the answers to questions like these are best found in the person of Jesus and what He could, and could not do.

Here's what I mean. In Matthew 13:54-14:1 it says, **"Jesus then came to his hometown, he began teaching the people in their synagogue, and they were amazed. 'Where did this man get this wisdom and these miraculous powers?' they asked. 'Isn't this the carpenter's son? Isn't his mother's name Mary, and aren't his brothers James, Joseph, Simon and Judas? Aren't all his sisters with us? Where then did this man get all these things?' And they took offense at him. But Jesus said to them, "Only in his hometown and in his own house is a prophet without honor." And <u>he could not do</u> many miracles there because of their lack of faith."**

Wait a minute... hold the phone! Jesus had times when He couldn't do miracles? Yes I realize He did some miracles, but "not many" means there were some that never happened. So what did Jesus do in instances when nothing happened? Did He question whether He Himself did not have enough faith? No. Did He question God's will and ability to do miracles? No. Did He lose His faith in the whole principle of walking by faith? No. Well if He didn't respond that way, then why does His Church?

Like Jesus, we need to understand that there are other factors involved in this faith walk. In this example, it was the lack of faith on the part of the other people.

An individual's personal faith is vital in the flow of God's power into their lives. Very much like electricity, God's power flows on the path of least resistance. Jesus is quoted many times saying, **"Your faith has healed you."** Or **"According to your faith it will be done."** Just like the woman with the issue of bleeding, she said, **"Even if I can only touch a piece of His clothes, I WILL be healed."**

And she was! Her own faith made her an open circuit for God's power to flow through her. Your own faith is what determines whether or not you have an open circuit for the flow of God's power through you.

Here's a hypothetical example: A Church receives news that one of their members is sick and dying. The whole Church of 1000 people could be praying and believing God for them to be healed, but if the individual themselves doesn't believe God heals, they will probably not get healed. And why would they? They don't even believe God heals! And they should believe, if they call themselves "a believer". Therefore there's resistance to the flow of the power of God, the people praying are connected to the power through faith, but the one who should receive is actually resisting. Jesus didn't lack the faith to perform miracles; the people lacked the faith to receive them. The circuit was closed. Electricity will stop, and not flow, at the point of utmost resistance.

I've also personally known of situations where the person believed in healing, but didn't want to be healed. They were just tired of this life, and wanted to go be with Jesus. And to be honest, I can't say I blame them. Even the Apostle Paul wanted to go be with the Lord, but chose to stay for the sake of Christ being proclaimed. If a person has lost the will to live this life, you can pray all you want for their healing and it's most likely not going to happen. God will not override their will, and neither should we think we can. That actually has to do with witchcraft. Witchcraft is about control and manipulation of another person's will. As the Church, we should have nothing to do with that.

We are not to use the power of manipulation; we are to use the power of agreement!

We are to agree together concerning the word of God to us and for us. There are many known reasons for faith blockages in a person's life: Bitterness, offense, unrepented hidden sin, lack of a will to live, or unbelief. Yet, however many that we know, there are times when we just don't know. That's why it's called faith. Remember, faith is trusting God even when you can't see or know why. We seem to forget this in the Church. We seem to think that we have to have all the answers. We seem to forget the chapter 11 Hebrews heroes of faith. **"They were all commended for their faith, yet none of them received what had been promised in their lifetime." (Verse 39)** Faith is not based on results; it is based on trusting God no matter what. Job knew this.

Even after God permitted Satan to take everything Job had, Job still said, **"Even if He slay me, yet I WILL trust Him." (Job 13:15)** And by the way, the reason God allowed Satan to do this, was to prove that people don't just serve God because of what He does for them, but because they love and trust Him. So what was really going on here, was that God was exalting Jobs' humility over Satan who fell from his original heavenly position because of pride! For then the Lord said to Satan, **"Have you considered my servant Job? There is no one on earth like him; he is blameless and upright, a man who fears God and shuns evil. (Job 2:3)** I love this, God was bragging about Job! God loves it when we trust and believe Him whether we see results or not!

The Bible is very clear in Hebrews 11:6 that, **"Without faith it is impossible to please God, because anyone who comes to him must believe that he exists and that he rewards those who earnestly seek him."** God loves it when no matter what happens, and no matter what anyone says, we believe in, and trust Him and what He has said He will do alone! Remember Abraham believed God before

Jason Silver

anything even happened, and it was accredited to him as righteousness. It doesn't say that he waited for the fulfillment of the promise before he believed God, no; God said it and Abraham believed it when He said it! That's faith! It doesn't demand results first, it demands trust and obedience. Just like the old song "Trust and obey, for there's no other way, to be happy in Jesus but to trust and obey."

Sometimes we miss out on what God wants to do, because we presume how He should do it.

Or He doesn't answer our prayer in the manner we thought it should have been answered. We find a perfect example of this in 2 Kings 5:11-14. The prophet's answer to Naaman's request for healing of leprosy was to go dip in the Jordan River seven times.

And this is how Naaman responded, **"But Naaman went away angry and said, "I thought that he would surely come out to me and stand and call on the name of the Lord his God, wave his hand over the spot and cure me of my leprosy. Are not Abana and Pharpar, the rivers of Damascus, better than any of the waters of Israel? Couldn't I wash in them and be cleansed?" So he turned and went off in a rage.**

Naaman's servant went to him and said, "My father, if the prophet had told you to do some great thing, would you not have done it? How much more, then, when he tells you, 'Wash and be cleansed'!" So he went down and dipped himself in the Jordan seven times, as the man of God had told him, and his flesh was restored and became clean like that of a young boy."

Fortunately Naaman chose to listen to the wisdom of his servant and was healed. But notice that he said "**I thought he would have…**" We must remember that it's up to us to ask, but up to God to answer.

And we should never presume how and when God should do something! Did you also notice that when the Prophet didn't do it the way Naaman thought he should have, Naaman went away angry? How many people in the Church are angry at God for not doing things the way they thought He should have? I tell you the truth, I've met many. And I've been guilty of it myself.

However, there's a principle I try to live by when it comes to this. And it is this: He is God and I am not, He knows things that I do not, therefore He leads and I must follow. Even when the way may not be fully in view. And I constantly remind myself that when I humble myself as Job did, God will exalt me at the right time. This He has promised us all. **"Humble yourselves, therefore, under God's mighty hand, that he may lift you up in due time." (1 Peter 5:6)**

We need to realize however that not everyone will receive Christ either, some will outright reject Him. You need to know this, so that it doesn't disappoint you in your faith to the point of giving up. Especially when it's a family member or someone you care about. They still have to make their own choice. Even Jesus came across those who refused to believe in Him. But He never gave up! So how do we deal with it?

In Acts 18:4-6 regarding the Apostle Paul it says that, **"Every Sabbath he reasoned in the synagogue, trying to persuade Jews and Greeks concerning salvation. When Silas and Timothy came from Macedonia, Paul devoted himself exclusively to preaching, testifying to the Jews that Jesus was the Christ. But when the Jews opposed Paul and became abusive, he shook out his clothes in protest and said to them, "Your blood be on your own heads! I am clear of my responsibility. From now on I will go to the Gentiles."**

So it's clear how we are to deal with the rejection of the Gospel, by moving on to others who will receive it. It's that simple. Even Jesus told us to shake the dust off our feet and move on. We can pray for them, but as far as proclamation goes, they don't want to hear it. I personally believe the Church today wastes a lot of time proclaiming the Gospel to people who don't really want to hear it. Some of these folks even attend Church, but it's only because they like the social aspect of fellowship with the people, it's not to be changed by the Gospel of Christ.

The Gospel of Jesus Christ was never meant to help us form social clubs; it was, and is meant to change our lives!

THE KINGDOM OF POWER

"For the kingdom of God is not a matter of talk but of power ." (1 Corinthians 4:20)

I really do believe that we are closer to the return of Christ than ever before. Things are going to heat up in the world more than ever before. And so will things in the Church! I believe that notable miracles will increase in frequency within the Church body. Meaning the people, not a building. Where we live, work, and play. Powerful and undeniable acts of God through His Church, that will not be refuted. I believe that the fear towards the Church that we see in the Book of Acts, will return because of the power that we will once again begin to operate in. And many will be added to our numbers. Exponential growth unlike anything we've ever seen before.

The world is tired of the Church's' talk. They're not listening anymore. It's going to take a power encounter to get their attention.

God will begin to show Himself strong once again. And all will know that He is God! I do not mean that all will accept Him, some still rejected Christ, but they were accountable for the miracles that they saw done among them.

Matthew 11:20 says...

"Then Jesus began to denounce the cities in which most of his miracles had been performed, because they did not repent."

Continued in Verse 23...

"If the miracles that were performed in you had been performed in Sodom, the city would have remained to this day."

Don't get me wrong, people are indeed accountable for what they hear when we as the Church share the truth. However, they are even more accountable when they actually see the truth demonstrated. All throughout the Gospel and the Book of Acts, it says that the people went about sharing what they SAW, and HEARD Jesus and the Disciples do. You see it's easy to deny what you've heard, but it's much harder to deny what you yourself have seen.

"And seeing the man who had been healed standing with them, they could say nothing against it. But when they had commanded them to go aside out of the council, they conferred among themselves, saying, "What shall we do to these men? For, indeed, that a notable miracle has been done through them is evident to all who dwell in Jerusalem, and we cannot deny it." (Acts 4:14-16)

Remember Thomas? He wouldn't even believe his beloved and trustworthy friends when they told him that Jesus was alive. **"Now Thomas, one of the Twelve, was not with the disciples when Jesus came. So the other disciples told him, "We have seen the Lord!"But he said to them, "Unless I see** the nail marks in his hands and put my finger where the nails were, and put my hand into his side, I will not believe it."

A week later his disciples were in the house again, and Thomas was with them. Though the doors were locked, Jesus came and stood among them and said, "Peace be with you!" Then he said to Thomas, "Put your finger here; see my hands. Reach out your hand and put it into my side. Stop doubting and believe."

Thomas said to him, "My Lord and my God!"

Then Jesus told him, "Because <u>you have seen me, you have believed</u>; blessed are those who have not seen and yet have believed."

<u>Jesus did many other miraculous signs</u> in the presence of his disciples, which are not recorded in this book. But <u>these are written that you may believe</u> that Jesus is the Christ, the Son of God, and that by believing you may have life in his name." (John 20:24-31)

Certainly the truth is what Jesus said, **"It's more blessed to believe even when you have not seen."** Because that actually takes more faith, and faith is pleasing to God. However, being that God is **"...not willing that any should be lost."** God will reveal Himself to others should He know they will believe, and be saved. There is no end to His kindness. And it's His kindness that "leads us to repentance."

I personally believe that God will do all He can to reach people in these last days. He's going to bring the world to the end of their rope, so that the only choices they have are to reach out for Him, or fall to their chosen demise. I believe He will stir up His Church, like never before, to reach the lost with the Good News of salvation in Jesus Christ alone! Call it the latter rain, coming revival, or whatever you want,

God will do it! We will see certain Church denominations working together that we never thought would, for the purpose of bringing in the harvest!

I mean, if the fields were ready for harvest in Jesus' day, how much more are they ready today?

Church, the road ahead of us will not be easy, but it will be powerful and exciting! So never forget these things, **"Greater is He that's in you, than he that's in the world."** And, **"The same power that raised Jesus from the dead lives in you."** And that you can do, **"...the very things that Jesus did"**, if you only believe in Him. So go out and freely give of what you have been freely given! Guard your faith and trust in God at all costs, hold fast to His written word in your hearts; and love one another deeply from your hearts and in humility, for this kind of love will never grow cold.

And if you're going to make mistakes, which you will, please make them by stepping out in faith and not by shrinking back in doubt and unbelief! Follow the examples of faith our forefathers laid out for us in scripture, and of those around you every day that live and walk by faith. If possible, mostly surround yourself with people of great faith, and avoid those who are unbelieving and hard hearted at all costs. You know what they say, "You can't soar with the eagles if you're pecking with the chickens."

Thank you for taking the time to read this book. I hope it leaves you feeling actively challenged, impassioned, and encouraged to walk in the same manner as Christ Himself did. I hope you don't just put it on the shelf when you're done, and forget the message that you've heard, but you act on it. And remember, don't wait for an Elijah to do something, be the Elijah.

I want to leave you with these encouraging words from the Apostle Paul. So be blessed and do the impossible with God!

Romans 15: 4 - 6

"For everything that was written in the past was written to teach us, so that through endurance and the encouragement of the Scriptures we might have hope. May the God who gives endurance and encouragement give you a spirit of unity among yourselves as you follow Christ Jesus, so that with one heart and mouth you may glorify the God and Father of our Lord Jesus Christ."

THE END

ABOUT THE AUTHOR

Jason is the husband to Patricia Silver and the father of three beautiful children Judah, Rebecca, and Cherith. Their family currently resides in Kimberley, British Columbia Canada. He is the Lead Pastor of Kimberley Foursquare Fellowship which he planted in 2006. He's been involved in ministry since the age of 15 years old knowing it was his life calling.

You can reach Jason in regards to ministry opportunities at the following web address below.

www.kimberleyfoursquare.com

Jason Silver

Made in the USA
Charleston, SC
16 April 2014